The Observer's Pocket Series

SMALL CRAFT

The Observer Books

The Observer's Book of

SMALL CRAFT

GORDON FAIRLEY

WITH OVER 260
ILLUSTRATIONS
IN THE TEXT AND
8 PAGES OF COLOUR PLATES

FREDERICK WARNE & CO LTD

FREDERICK WARNE & CO INC

LONDON: NEW YORK

AUTHOR'S NOTE

The author makes no apology for including large sailing vessels in a book of 'small craft', bearing in mind that these days the majority are sailed for pleasure by 'small craft operators'. What does the sailor of today call himself? Certainly not an 'amateur' for he is closer to the sea than many a professional.

Library of Congress Catalog No.
76-2925

ISBN 0 7232 1559 6

Printed in Great Britain by
Butler & Tanner Ltd, Frome and London
744.676

CONTENTS

ACKNOWLEDGMENTS

The Author is grateful for the assistance of many manufacturers, yacht brokers, Class Owners' Associations, other organizations and individuals: To Brian Watson for his care and interest in producing the line drawings; to *Yachts and Yachting* magazine for searching their records for a number of the photographs; to a number of colleagues and friends (especially Charles Currey on the powerboat section of the book) for their criticism, always helpful and constructive, and to his wife, Joanna, for her help with the manuscript and typing, and for her toleration of the Postman's knock, the telephone and the Author while the book was in preparation!

He also gives grateful thanks to the following photographers, companies and organizations who have kindly given their permission to reproduce photographs in this book. Figures in **heavy** type refer to the black and white photographs which are numbered throughout the text: Albin Marine for **58**; Anstey Yachts, **124**; Nick Armstrong, **155, 162, 163**; Australian News and Information Bureau, **161**; John Baker (Kenton Forge) Ltd, **112**; J.S. Biscoe, **76**; Alistair Black, Pl. 5 (above); A. Bromley Martin, **4** and Pl. 3 (above); J. Broughton, **168**; Camper and Nicholsons Ltd, **96, 99**; Carter Offshore Yachts, **63**; Central Office of Information, **41**; Frank Chapman, **185, 203, 207**; Robert Chapman, **246**; Cheverton Boats Ltd, **221, 222**; C-Lark Association, **178**; M. Cocking, **150**; Comextra Ltd, **82**; Continental Yacht Agency, **102, 103, 111**; Peter Copley, **191, 195**; Corporation of Trinity House, **35, 36, 37, 38**; Trevor Davies, **68, 123, 204**; D.P.N., **171**; Michel Dufour, **53**; Jonathan Eastland, **28, 29, 30, 31, 34, 78, 141, 142, 146, 147, 148, 211, 213, 232** and Pl. 2 (above and below), Pl. 3 (below), Pl. 4 (above and centre), Pl. 5 (below), Pl. 6 (both photos), Pl. 7 (all photos); Enterprise Association, **153**; John Etches, **59**; Fairey Marine Ltd, **174**; Ambrose Greenway, **79**; Gull Class Association, **187**; H.M. Coastguard, **47**; Jack Holt Ltd, **196**; Honnor Marine Ltd, **179, 180, 181**; Gina Hunt, **184**; B.J. de la Hunty (Marine) Ltd, **128**; International Tornado Class Association, **169**; D. Edmund Jones, **149, 150, 151, 154, 156, 159, 160, 165, 177, 186, 189, 194**; Kingfisher Yachts, **83, 85**; K.N.Z.H.R.M., **44**; Anthony J.

Linton, **54, 55, 56, 57, 228, 230;** Kim Loxby, **166;** Macwester Marine Co. Ltd, **87, 88;** Brian Manby, **62, 66, 67, 81, 101, 119, 120, 121, 198;** Marcon (U.K.) Ltd, **89, 110;** Roger Nadal, **190;** National 12 Class Association, **208;** Nautor, **118, 122;** Northshore Yacht Agencies, **219;** N.S.C.O.A., **201;** the *Observer* newspaper, **43;** Offshore Yachts International Ltd, **91;** Cdr. James O'Sullivan, U.S.C.G., Pl. 2 (centre); Michael Pocock and Partners, **105;** Ian Proctor, **202;** Eileen Ramsay, **175, 206, 231;** R.N.L.I., **42, 43** and Pl. 4 (centre); Russell Marine Ltd, **52, 127;** Rydgeway Marine Ltd, **106, 107;** Sea Cadet Corps, **7;** Skyfotos, England, **40;** Small Craft (Blockley) Ltd, **108;** Southern Ocean Shipyard Ltd, **33, 78;** South Hants Marine Ltd, **113, 114;** F.E. Sparkes Marine Ltd, **65, 71, 72, 75, 109;** Vernon Stratton, **167;** Studio 77, **210;** U.S. Coastguard, **45, 46;** Wayfarer Class Association, **209;** Westerly Marine Construction Ltd, **129, 137;** *Yachting World*, **93.**

Chapter 1

INTRODUCTION TO SAIL

The observer of sailing boats is observing history. A boat that the Polynesians invented some 7000 years ago is, today, considered to be 'the latest design'.

The practical history of man's struggle to use an alien element—to venture upon the waters of the deep—is part of 'observation'. He observed, and he learned and he evolved new designs.

How it all began

While the Egyptians (who were good at recording their history) were building boats and sails from papyrus reeds and strips of acacia, men in Northern Europe were making coracles or something similar. The boats had no keels and seldom more than a 'square' sail with which to blow before the wind.

About 2000 B.C. the Minoans of Crete, being desperate to trade with others, did so in boats cut out of tree trunks, which were then built up with planks laid edge to edge, now known as 'carvel' built. At a much later date the Norsemen or Vikings developed the stronger method of construction known as 'clinker-built' (where the planks overlap each other for greater strength). As their boats got larger and they themselves more adventurous, more power was needed than could be provided by muscles and oars. It is the Vikings who are thought to have been the first to consider rigging their ships so that the sails could be turned to face the oncoming wind. However there were many sorts of craft evolving in the Mediterranean countries. It soon became general knowledge that the triangular sail was best for work close to the direction of the wind, and the four-sided sail for catching the maximum amount of wind when strong following winds were blowing.

Between the 15th and 17th centuries there were enormous improvements in the shape and design of vessels for making war or trading. Most vessels were equipped with square sails but increasing numbers were designed with fore-and-aft sails evolved from the 'lateen' triangular sails used in such vessels as the 'carrack'. The *Santa Maria*, the ship in which Columbus sailed, was rigged like that. Such a vessel could have two to four masts. A square 'spritsail' was rigged in the bow to steady the ship's head. The fore and main masts would be square-rigged and the after-mast (called the mizzen-mast) would be rigged with a fore-and-aft sail.

Fore-and-aft sails

Later, vessels were rigged with more fore-and-aft sails. The headsails were rigged to a jib-boom (a spar projecting from the bowsprit in the bow of the vessel). The full-rigged ships of the line, such as the 102-gun *H.M.S. Victory* (which was built at the Chatham Dockyard between 1759 and 1765), would be accompanied by faster vessels with big headsails, frigates, corvettes and sloops. In those days the sloop, which was a fast warship, smaller than a corvette, was used for fast passage-making and for such high speed and arduous jobs as the hunting and catching of smugglers! In later years the sloop evolved from a vessel carrying a considerable spread of square-rigged sails (on three masts) into a single-masted fore-and-aft rigged ship. The final evolution is the Bermudan-rigged sloop of today with both working sails rigged fore-and-aft. Compared to square-riggers, the sails are easier to handle and need fewer crew.

Along the years many strange vessels have been constructed, mainly for the cargo-carrying world. The British East Indiaman *Essex* spread a full set of sixty-three sails. On her mainmast she carried twenty-one sails, including three set above the sky-sail—a 'cloudscraper', a 'moonraker' and a 'star-gazer'! The drawing on page 12 gives some indication of the number and variety of sails.

Another famous vessel is recalled by many who saw her sailing only just before World War II: the *Cutty Sark*, on a grain race from Australia, cutting up the channel into Falmouth, every sail set with a crew of only twenty, many of them boys! She now occupies a dry dock at Greenwich, England.

Trading Ships

France claims the distinction of building the largest sailing vessel. The *France* was a five-masted steel barque with an overall length of 127·4m (418ft). Carrying her incredible 10,870m² (13,000yd²) of sail, she was eventually torpedoed in 1917.

Another vessel to create a record was the American vessel *Thomas W. Lawson*. She was the only seven-masted schooner ever built. Her masts were 59·4m (195ft) from truck to deck, the top part being wooden and the lower part steel. Her total sail area was only 33,816m² (4444yd²) but her seven masts made her something special.

Right up to 1939 there were quite a large number of sailing ships trading for profit. Even more recently the *Pamir* was sailing 1000 miles out of Buenos Aires when she was caught by the tail of a hurricane—in September 1957 the sea claimed one more victim and the majority of the lives of the thirty-five sailors and fifty-one cadets. Her sister ship, the *Passat*, is now moored in the harbour of Travemunde where, like many other famous sailing ships, she serves to remind visitors of the strength and grace of the sailing ships, the dangers and joys of 'making sail' to far distant places, and the men who did it.

1: A diagrammatic drawing of a full-rigged ship

1. The bow
2. The stern
3. The 'after-part' of the ship
4. The jib boom
5. The bowsprit
6. The dolphin striker (providing the downward lead for the jib-boom martingales—guys to stop the jib boom lifting)
7. The flying jib
8. The outer jib
9. The inner jib
10. The foremast
11. The fore course
12. The fore lower topsail
13. The fore upper topsail
14. The fore topgallant (pronounced to gallant)
15. The fore royal
16. The main course (or mainsail)
17. The main lower topsail
18. The main upper topsail
19. The main topgallant
20. The main royal
21. The skysail
22. The mizzen (a fore-and-aft sail

hoisted on the mizzen-mast. It is sometimes called the 'spanker' or 'driver' but never the mizzensail)
23. The cross jack (pronounced cro'jack). The sail is called the mizzen course and is shown furled. The cross jack is the name of the yard itself
24. The mizzen lower topsail
25. The mizzen upper topsail
26. The mizzen topgallant
27. The mizzen royal

The sails marked with an A are all studding sails (pronounced stunsails). These are 'extended' out to the sides to set at the outer edges of the square sails in order to extend the sail area even further.

The sails marked with an S are called staysails. There may be almost any number of such staysails which are named from the stay upon which they are hanked, e.g. forestaysail.

12

Chapter 2

'TALL SHIPS' TODAY

Even today, the keen observer may see many square-rigged sailing vessels in commission, apart from a number of 'museum' ships. Most of those in commission are used for sail training. If you ever have the chance to watch a gathering of these craft, you should be able to identify the different rigs from this book. First, you will realize that every 'ship' is not just a ship, and every 'yacht' is not just a yacht. The big ones may be full-rigged ships, or barques, barquentines, schooners etc. The yachts may be sloops, ketches, yawls, or cutters, either gaff or Bermudan-rigged.

So, before we go any further with the business of observing and identifying, we must supply the information so that you may accurately describe the craft that you see. Right down to the most modern of sailing craft, the vocabulary of the sea has altered very little. Careful study of the illustrations which

2: A full-rigged ship showing sail plan, starboard ratlines and a maze of running rigging

13

follow will be rewarding, and will add to your general knowledge.

A Full-rigged Ship has all masts square-rigged. In illustration **2** (which is an artist's impression of the Danish ship the *Danmark*) you can identify the mizzen, and no fewer than *seven* staysails. The 'front' four triangular sails are known as the jib topsail, the flying jib, the outer jib and the inner jib. The last of the five would be called a forestaysail, which, with the three between each mast, makes the seven staysails. Strictly speaking the flying jib should not be hanked on a stay but, nowadays, the practice is to set all headsails on a stay.

3: An artist's impression of a Barque showing sail plan and part of the rigging

3 is an artist's impression of a **Barque**. A barque may be a three, four or five-masted vessel with all masts square-rigged except the aftermost which is rigged fore-and-aft. Examples of such craft still sailing today are the German *Gorch Fock* built in 1958 with a sail area of 1952m² (21,011ft²). The American vessel *Eagle* (Pl. 2) which belongs to the United States Coastguard is also a three-masted barque, built in the same shipyard (Blohm and Voss of Hamburg). The Russian vessel *Tovarisch* is another example. She was the original *Gorch Fock* built in the early 1900s. She is now used by the Russian Merchant Navy as a training ship.

A Barquentine (not illustrated) is a vessel of three, four or five masts, but only the foremast will be rigged with square sails.

A Schooner is a fore-and-aft rigged vessel with two or more masts. If she has only two masts the after mast will be no shorter than the foremast (otherwise she would be called a ketch or yawl). A schooner can be more precisely described (and identified) by the terms 'topsail' schooner, 'staysail' schooner or 'gaff' schooner etc. The *Sir Winston Churchill*

4: The *Sir Winston Churchill* is owned by the British Sail Training Association

5: A Three-masted Staysail Schooner

(**4,** and Pl. 3) has a sister ship the *Malcolm Miller*. Both belong to the British Sail Training Association and are topsail schooners. They are identical, except in very minor details. Like many of the 'tall ships', they have been built recently. Both were designed by Camper and Nicholsons Ltd and have a tonnage of 299 tons Thames. There is a permanent crew of eleven, including eight officers and the ships carry forty-four cadets.

Most if not all of the 'tall ships' actually sailing with cadets on board were built no later than 1930 and they are all equipped with sizable engines. In this respect they differ from the originals which, of course, had no engines. It is, however, necessary to ensure the safety of the ship and for that reason engines are now installed.

The line illustration above shows the possible sail plan of a **Three-masted Staysail Schooner.**

The 197 tons *Zawoska Czarny*, a Polish vessel which carries a full complement of forty-five crew, twenty-five being cadets, is another example of a recently built three-masted staysail schooner. She was built in 1952 at Danzig and has taken part in a number of the 'tall ships' races.

The illustration **6** depicts the *Gladan*, one of two sister ships which belong to the Royal Swedish Navy. The other, the *Falken*, was built in 1946 and the *Gladan* in 1947.

6: The *Gladan*, a Two-masted Gaff Schooner

One of the prerequisites for the modern 'tall ship' is that it should not be too difficult to work, bearing in mind that the crews change at very frequent intervals and, in many cases, have never been on board such a vessel before.

7: The British Training Brig *Royalist* built by the Sea Cadet Corps to give offshore training in square-rigged vessels

A Brig is illustrated in **7**: a two-masted vessel with square sails on both masts and a gaff mainsail. A gaff is the spar to which the head of a fore-and-aft mainsail is 'bent on' (attached). This attachment may be by knots known as 'bends' (to distinguish them from 'hitches') or, in more modern vessels, by slides in a groove.

A Brigantine (not illustrated) is rather similar but has square sails on the foremast only, being fore-and-aft rigged on the main.

The schooner rig in its various forms was evolved to produce a vessel capable of making passage in areas where the winds were not always favourable. The

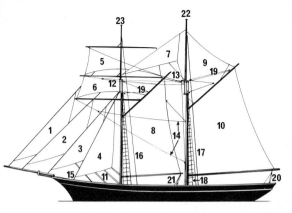

8: A Two-masted Topsail Schooner

1. Flying Jib
2. Outer jib
3. Inner jib
4. Foresail
5. Fore upper topsail
6. Fore lower topsail
7. Main topmast staysail
8. Foresail
9. Main gaff topsail
10. Mainsail
11. Jib and forestaysail sheets
12. Lower topsail braces
13. Upper topsail braces
14. Fore braces
15. Forestay (to support the mast)

16. Fore topmast backstay
17. Main topmast backstay
18. Shrouds with ratlines (cross lines rigged on the shrouds to form ladders to go aloft). 15, 16, 17 and 18 are known as 'the standing rigging' and support the masts. Sheets and halyards, to haul in or haul up the sails, are known as 'running rigging'
19. Halyards
20. Mainsheet
21. Foresheet
22. Mainmast
23. Foremast

square-sailed ships depended so much on such winds that they were often in difficulty in making fast passage. The schooners, on the other hand, were able to sail much closer to the wind and had the other advantage of requiring less crew to hand the sails. As in the modern yacht, the great advantage of the schooner is that the majority of the sails may be adjusted by hauling in or letting out the 'sheet' attached to the lower after corner of the boom. In the square-rigged ship it is necessary to 'brace' the yards round when the sail needs adjustment. A further advantage of the schooner is that the majority of the sails can be set without sending men aloft.

The diagrammatic illustration on page 19 of a **Two-masted Topsail Schooner** will more clearly depict the advantages of this type of rig. It also shows many features of the sailing vessel which have not changed to this day. What have changed most dramatically are the materials used for sailing vessels. In the days of Nelson the ropes and the blocks through which they passed were of natural materials. The blocks, made of wood, had to be enormous to stand the strain and to carry the thick 'manilla' rope of which all cordage was made. The hulls, even of the hardest wood, were prey to marine parasites and deterioration caused by the elements. With the advent of man-made materials, such as glass-reinforced polyester for hulls; nylon, terylene and polypropylene for ropes; and various new materials for blocks, the size of all equipment (including the standing rigging to hold up the masts) has radically diminished. Some of the 'tall ships' of today have been designed to make use of these new materials.

Chapter 3

MODERN SAILING CRAFT

9: A Bermudan Sloop with tall triangular sails. Note the modern 'overlap' of the head sail

The majority of craft are now fore-and-aft rigged.

Gaff rig is where the head of the fore-and-aft mainsail is bent on to a spar. In a **Bermudan Sloop,** the mainsail is tall and triangular. The head of the mainsail goes to the masthead, and the foot to a boom (a spar extending the foot of the mainsail). The luff (front edge of the sail) is kept to the mast by setting the luff rope in a groove or by slides in a track running up the mast.

10: A Gaff Sloop with the mainsail on a top spar called the 'gaff' and a bottom spar called the 'boom'

21

In a **gunter rig** (**11**) the sail is bent on to the gaff, which is slung from a strop about two-thirds of the way along its length. Note that the sail is actually a four-sided sail, while the Bermudan sloop mainsail is three-sided.

11 : A Gunter-rigged Sloop with four-sided mainsail

Another rather difficult piece of identification, which becomes easier with practice, is the distinction between a **Ketch** and a **Yawl.** As will be seen in illustrations **12** and **13,** a ketch is a two-masted sailing vessel with a large mizzen-mast stepped well forward of the rudder. A yawl, on the other hand, although being a similar vessel, has a much smaller mizzen-mast stepped aft of the rudder post. This mast carries a much smaller mizzen. Both the ketch and the yawl rig make the handling of sails and the manoeuvrability of the craft easier.

12: A Bermudan Ketch with the mizzen-mast well forward

13: A Bermudan Yawl with a small mizzen-mast stepped well aft

Compare the **Bermudan Ketch, 12,** with the **Gaff Ketch, 14,** and also the difference between the **Gaff Yawl, 15,** and the **Bermudan Yawl, 13.**

It will be obvious to the observer that the few craft already discussed are by no means all that will be seen. Apart from the smaller open boats which are discussed later we must complete the picture of what may be seen in the way of the different types of rig used in the larger sailing boats.

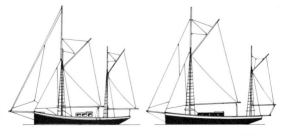

14: A Gaff Ketch   **15**: A Gaff Yawl

23

Like the Bermudan sloop, the **Cutter** has a single mast but carries two working headsails. She will carry a jib, which may be set up on the topmast stay or may be set on a stay between the topmast stay and the forestay. A cutter with a short overhang on the bow may need, like the ships of olden days, a bowsprit to allow a sufficiently large spread of sail and to prevent the jib from overlapping the staysail too much.

Since a large number of the more modern sailing craft are rigged as **Bermudan Cutters,** and carry no bowsprit, **16** depicts a craft which may be seen on many occasions.

Compare illustration **9,** a Bermudan sloop, with either **16** or **17,** both of which are Bermudan-rigged cutters.

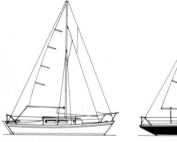 

16: A Bermudan Cutter

17: A Bermudan Cutter with a bowsprit

Naturally there are many good reasons for the variation in rigs. The commonest is that the designer finds it convenient to give the vessel smaller headsails. Equally, for reasons of convenience of sail setting, many cruising boats carry two headsails.

18: A Gaff Cutter with topsail

Apart from the Bermudan cutters, it is likely that the occasional **Gaff Cutter** will be seen. Note the gaff topsail in illustration **18.**

Unfortunately, however, it is not always correct to assume that a vessel setting two headsails will automatically be called a cutter. **19** depicts a **Gaff Yawl.** Although she carries two headsails she is known as a

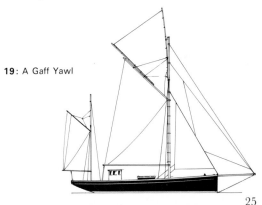

19: A Gaff Yawl

gaff yawl because she has a four-sided mainsail supported at the head by a spar. She rates as a yawl because of the small mizzen set aft of the rudder post. Equally if she had a mizzen-mast with a larger mizzen placed forward of the rudder post she would be called a **Gaff Ketch.**

Reefing

If the wind grows stronger all sailing vessels will need to shorten sail. To continue in a strong blow with the maximum sail set is courting disaster. Also the vessel will be pressed over on her side and she will lose efficiency as a sailing boat. The judgment as to whether a craft is carrying too much sail depends, to a certain extent, on whether she is heeled over too far and therefore has only a small portion of her hull in the water.

Headsails may be reduced in size and in fore-and-aft rigged craft the mainsail will also be lowered slightly and the lower part of the sail secured to the boom. This may be achieved either by using the modern equipment known as roller reefing (where the boom can be turned over and the sail 'rolled' on to it) or by gathering the sail in 'slabs' and securing it to the boom.

20: A Bermudan Sloop reefed well down for bad weather conditions. Failure to reef as the wind gets stronger may result in the loss of the mast

Rigging and sails

The majority of the terms used for the parts of a modern sailing craft originated from the terms used in the old sailing ships.

The masts of any sailing vessel naturally need to be supported because of the enormous pressure exerted by the wind on the sails, quite apart from the actual weight of the spars and sails.

The rigging line supporting the mast, which runs from the topmast to the bow, is called the 'forestay'. The sail which was attached to this stay took its name from the stay—thus we have 'forestaysail'. A sail set away out on the end of the bowsprit or the jib-boom (an extension of the bowsprit) in an old sailing craft would, however, be known as the 'jib' even though it was hanked on to a stay. If the headsail of a modern sloop is set from the end of the bowsprit it would therefore follow that it should be called a 'jib', but if it is set on a stay from a point inboard of the bow (the stemhead) it would more correctly be called a 'forestaysail'. The word has become shortened in use to 'foresail' but it is more correct to speak of a 'headsail'. The common usage nowadays is to call a single headsail a 'jib' and, if there are two headsails, the inner will be called 'the staysail'.

As a result of considerable experimentation it was discovered, quite early on in the development of the modern yacht, that the size of the headsail could be increased until its leech (the back edge) came well aft of the mast. The observer will see many of the older craft with quite small headsails but the more modern the yacht, the larger the headsail and the smaller the mainsail. These large headsails are called 'genoas' (frequently corrupted to 'Jenny'). In fair weather the skipper of a yacht will select this sail to provide maximum speed and a good 'balanced' rig.

The mast must also be supported from falling forward and for this purpose a 'backstay' is rigged from the top of the mast to the stern. In some craft twin backstays will be fitted and these will not run directly to a centrepoint on the stern but to either side of the craft, near the stern. In certain Bermudan-rigged yachts, depending on the length of the boom, these backstays are fitted to runners so that the one on the leeward (the side away from the wind) can be slackened off. It it were not, the boom and sail would hit it.

Finally the 'shrouds' on either side of the craft stop the mast from falling sideways.

The forestay, backstay and shrouds are known as the 'standing rigging' and any movable line as 'running rigging'.

When a mainsail is set the boom is supported by the sail. However when the craft is not sailing, the after end of the boom, unless it has support, would drop into the cockpit. The observer will see a line running from near the masthead to the after end of the boom. This will be taut when no sail is set and slackened off when under sail. This line is appropriately called the 'topping lift'.

Not so visible to the observer will be all the lines used to raise the sails towards the masthead. These are called 'halyards' and run through blocks near the masthead. When a sail needs to be set, the halyard is attached to the sail and the sail pulled up from the deck. The crew do not need to go aloft.

In the old sailing ships the square-rigged sails were already set on spars and it was a question of going aloft to loose them from their fastenings. The triangular sails would all be raised by means of halyards and manpower! Nowadays the halyards and other moving rigging in the larger boats are passed round geared winches which means that far less crew (and effort!) is required to hoist sails. Even in quite small boats the amount of sail is sufficient to require a winch to assist the crewmen to hoist or 'sheet in' sail.

Once a sail has been set it is necessary to control it so that it will fill with wind and drive the sailing craft along. Merely to hoist sail would be insufficient.

Special modern sails

Since the object in any yacht race is to win, and winning necessitates sailing fast, the setting of sufficient sail is of vital importance. At the same time, to set too much sail may heel the yacht over so far that she becomes an inefficient machine.

The observer cannot fail to notice a yacht when a spinnaker is set. This is another form of headsail which is very light, very large, usually multi-coloured and balloon shaped. It acts exactly like an umbrella on a windy day and is set, when the yacht is running before the wind, on the opposite side to the mainsail.

There are various shapes of spinnaker for use in varying conditions of wind, some being cut to be most effective when the wind is not coming from *dead* astern.

These spinnakers are, to some extent, a continuation of the old idea of square sails but are designed to be worked from the deck and cockpit. The foot of the sail is restrained by a sheet (rope) at one corner and a guy attached to the outboard end of a boom, at the other. When the sail is hoisted the angle it makes to the wind is controlled by slackening and tightening the sheet and guy. Additionally this sail may be augmented by other specially cut headsails. The modern 'Tallboy' is a very slim tall headsail which fits between the mast and the spinnaker. The 'Big Boy' (which is not hanked on to a stay) fits alongside the spinnaker to add to the sail area.

Nearly every class of racing yacht, however small, uses a spinnaker while racing but, naturally, only when running before, or nearly before, the wind. So this is why racing yachts, as they reach a certain mark of the course, will be seen to strike or raise their spinnakers according to the wind direction.

However, these rather special sails do not in any way alter the designation of the various types of sailing boat which have specific descriptions according to the style of their rig.

Smaller craft

We have described the various rigs which you may see in 'tall ships' and offshore craft. In fact the observer on the seashore is more likely to see the craft which are now described because they are all the small dayboat rigs.

We use the word **Dayboat,** meaning either a dinghy (which has a retractable centreplate, centreboard or daggerboard to act as a keel) or a **Keelboat** (which has a fixed keel).

Both the **Bermudan sloop** rig and the **gunter rig** are employed extensively in both dayboats and yachts because both rigs are easy to handle. Particularly note the accentuated drawing of the gaff jaws in the craft in illustration **22**. The mainsail is *four*-sided. This rig

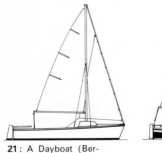

21: A Dayboat (Bermudan sloop-rigged)

22: A Dayboat (Gunter-rigged)

23: A Gaff-rigged
Dayboat

24: A Dayboat with
lugsail

is very popular for 'car top' dinghies because the spars
are not too long to stow on the roof of the car.

Notice the difference between **23** and **24**. The gaff-
rigged dayboat has no part of the mainsail in front
of the mast. The lugsail is quite different.

25 and **26** are of historical interest, being direct
descendants of ancient rigs. The craft in **25** has a
sprit which is a boom or spar set diagonally across
a sail from the mast to the peak. The **lateen** sail
depicted in **26** was used by Christopher Columbus
and also in the 9th century in the Mediterranean.

25: A Spritsail-
rigged Dayboat

26: A Lateen-rigged
Dayboat where the sail
is bent to the yard set
obliquely to the mast

Chapter 4

WIND AND WATER

Having read so far, the observer might imagine that sailing vessels go in the direction in which the wind takes them. This is not so. The only direction in which a skipper cannot *choose* to go is dead into the wind. He must, however, adjust his sails to suit the direction of the wind in relation to his course. Sailing almost into the wind, he must sail close-hauled very slightly *across* it, then turn and sail across it again. A zig-zag course known as 'tacking'.

Down-wind sailing is easy, except that the wind is never quite constant and may cause trouble if it gets round behind the sail! Hence, the prudent mariner chooses to sail *slightly* across the wind direction.

If the course required is at right-angles to the wind, this is known as reaching.

27 depicts a sloop-rigged yacht (but the *principle* is

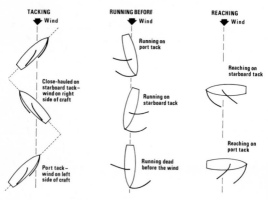

27: The various 'points of sailing'

exactly the same for a square-rigged ship). Both crew and helmsman will slack off or tighten the ropes controlling the sails (known as 'sheets') as occasion demands and according to the direction of the wind in relation to the course they wish to steer.

Forces acting on a boat's hull

The provision of some sort of a keel, either a movable centreboard or centreplate, or a fixed keel is essentially to stop the sailing boat 'skidding' sideways.

What other effects are there on a boat? The current in a river and the tidal stream on the sea. As the tide ebbs and flows, so the tidal streams gather speed and the big ships sail on the tide—when the tide is flowing to their advantage—to hurry them on their way.

Tidal ebb and flow and wind

Lastly it may help to know that when the wind is blowing against the direction of the tide the water will always be much rougher. Even if the mariner has no tidal atlas, he can tell from various signs which way the tide is flowing. He may look at moored boats which normally tend to lie to their moorings with their bows facing the direction in which the tide is moving. He will look at buoys, or mooring piles to see which side the tide is 'piling up'. From this he can tell again which way the tide is going—ebbing or flooding. He hardly needs to notice the direction in which flags etc are fluttering. Wind speed and direction are noted automatically.

No seagull ever stands facing down-wind. Imagine the result! In fact, if you start thinking about it, even a person who has never been near a boat notices the wind, not for the reasons of the mariner but as a considerable nuisance if it is blowing in his face and not so much of a nuisance if it is not. To a mariner, it is his fuel, his motive power and, in days of old, his livelihood.

Chapter 5

THE EVOLUTION OF SAILING FOR SPORT

The first 'pleasure yachts'

There are many claims to the distinction of being the 'first' pleasure yacht. In Great Britain the Royal pleasure vessels of Charles II were racing purely for pleasure in the 1660s. The King and his brother built some twenty-six vessels which resembled miniature frigates, after the style of many Dutch vessels, from which language the word 'yacht' is taken.

Although, no doubt, people were racing boats for pleasure in the United States of America before 1816, the historians relate that *Cleopatra's Barge*, built for one George Crowninshield, was the first true craft built solely for pleasure. The owner cruised her to the Mediterranean and back home to Salem in 1817. She was fitted out with chandeliers, mahogany furniture, velvet and gold curtains etc!

The first yacht clubs

The formation of yacht clubs began in the 18th century with the Water Club of Cork Harbour (1720) which later became the Royal Cork Yacht Club.

The Cumberland Fleet (the forerunner of the Royal Thames Yacht Club) was formed in 1749. A club in Cowes (Isle of Wight) became the Royal Yacht Club when the Prince Regent, who was already a member, came to the throne in 1820. In 1833 it became the world famous Royal Yacht Squadron. Meanwhile, across the Atlantic, sailing gentlemen in New York were forming themselves into the New York Yacht Club, which event took place in 1844.

In August 1851 Commodore John C. Stevens

brought the schooner *America* to England, won the Royal Yacht Squadron's Cup from the club and took it back to America. The cup became the trophy for the famous America's Cup Race.

How yacht racing evolved

Any observer of the yachting scene can hardly have failed to notice that a number of different sizes of yachts race against each other. To understand what is being observed, and how yacht racing evolved will undoubtedly enhance the interest. The challenge for the America's Cup (as it is now called) was, in a way, the beginning of a whole breed of people—the yacht racers. Racing is now the sport of tens of thousands in many parts of the world, in many different sizes of vessel. In Britain races for small boats were organized by the Royal Yacht Squadron as early as the 1890s. These could be crewed by the owner and one or more friends. The huge racers of a displacement of up to 150 tons began to give place to craft right down to 3·7m (12ft) in length. The introduction of man-made materials, for hulls and sails, rather than wood and cotton, made craft much cheaper and so the 'yachting explosion' gathered force. The majority of smaller dayboats race against other similar craft built to strict 'Class Rules'. The larger boats, although differing in design, are measured and handicapped against each other by a variety of systems which have been expanded, enlarged, and even radically altered over the years. The 'rating' which they receive from the official racing measurers is a complicated admixture of hull and sail measurements. To put it at its simplest, a mariner may give away a point or two on his handicap if his sail area exceeds the limits, but the fact that the hull of his vessel is smaller than the next man's may give him 'points' in his favour. In the section on 'Dayboats (Centreboard and Keelboat)' many of those illustrated are raced as strictly One-Design classes. In the 'Sailing Cruisers and Offshore Racers' section many will be racing against vessels different in design but within a maximum limit for the particular 'Class'. The Offshore Rating Council, set up by the common consent of yachtsmen from many different countries, and the International Yacht Racing Union, which was formed in 1906, between them see to the rules for all international racing, and each country has its national governing body.

The history of the One Ton Cup and the classes derived from it started in 1898 when it was presented by members of the Cercle de la Voile de Paris. It was essentially for small inshore keelboats and was sailed for a number of years as a match race between France and Great Britain. In 1906 the 'international rule' was created by the newly formed International Yacht Racing Union (I.Y.R.U.) for a whole range of yachts at a fixed rating from 5m to 23m in length.

28: Ocean racers competing in the Cowes to Dinard race. Note the 'National' letters. The leading yacht is from Argentina, the second from the United Kingdom and the third from Belgium

Eventually the cup was put up for a competition between yachts of 22ft (Royal Ocean Racing Club rating) but without time allowance. The same principle is now used for smaller 'classes', resulting in the present number of 'level rating' classes. The Half Ton and Quarter Ton Cups were originated by the French for European-owned yachts and the International Offshore Rating Council nominated the Two Ton and Three-Quarter Ton Cups in 1972. All these cups are for 'offshore races'.

In all classes, racing and the design of boats are, of course, closely connected. During the 1960s and 1970s materials and methods of construction, particularly design and interior layout of craft, have forged ahead. The modern ocean racer is a racing machine; while at the same time quite a number of designs cater for the cruising man. The increase in the number of yacht harbours and the facilities which they offer have also created a social change from the days when a yachtsman would take his 'cruiser' racing. Some of the latest models of racing offshore craft are equipped solely for racing with no pretensions to comfort below. On the other hand many sailing cruisers have central heating (the sort of luxury unheard of until the 1970s).

The competition between countries is intense, and perhaps most intense in the very big ocean racers.

The selection of teams for the Admiral's Cup series is established over a series of races and ultimately each country selects three vessels to compete. As has been mentioned already, these craft race against each other under an international rule of measurement and in many cases the vessels are 'one-off' designs.

In the smaller classes, Half and Quarter Ton Cup craft, many started out as a design for a small cruiser, with racing potential, but have been found to be so competitive, and fast, that they have 'emerged' and increased in number as a result of their racing capability.

29: *Saga* and *Salty Goose* in close competition

Illustration **29** shows two ocean racers competing against each other on the down-wind leg of a course. These races are usually around the 300-mile mark, keeping the yachts at sea for lengthy periods. However these craft will also race close within sight of land, especially at such international gatherings as Cowes Week, which is held during the

30: *Dictator,* a One Ton Cup competitor

first week in August, when yachts race through and out of the Solent, between the port of Southampton and the Isle of Wight. The two illustrations, *Dictator* (**30**) and *Sabina* (**31**), depict very clearly the differences which may exist in design. Note the entirely different shapes of their sterns which, of course, mean that the underwater configuration will be entirely different. Both these craft are in the One Ton category, and can be handled, as can be seen in the illustrations, by five or six men. The larger ocean racers may carry a crew of ten or eleven people. All are equipped to a very high standard of safety, with everything which may be needed in an emergency; all are raced to their maximum capacity and all, of course, carry as much sail as can be set.

In the following pages many different sorts of cruisers and offshore racers have been selected for discussion. With constantly changing designs and improvements, the book contains by no means all the craft which you will see but a selection of the most interesting or most popular.

31 : *Sabina*, under press of sail, shows her stern, and true racing shape

Chapter 6

MODERN DESIGN AND CONSTRUCTION

The design of offshore craft, fully decked except for a cockpit area for the crew, depends, to a very large extent, on whether the designer was intending to produce an out-and-out racing machine, or a cruiser, or a mixture of both.

The underwater lines of vessels are all-important and nowadays most designs are tested in model form in tanks.

Hulls and moulds

For mass production the shape of the hull is then made in wood and a mould made of the construction. From this original almost any number of identical hulls can be made in glass-reinforced polyester (G.R.P.). Sheets of glassfibre of varying thicknesses are set up in the mould with resins and gel coat (to form the smooth exterior of the hull). The superstruc-

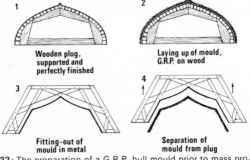

1 Wooden plug, supported and perfectly finished

2 Laying up of mould, G.R.P. on wood

3 Fitting-out of mould in metal

4 Separation of mould from plug

32: The preparation of a G.R.P. hull mould prior to mass production

ture, deck and cockpit area, is usually moulded in a separate mould and the hull is then joined to the deck. While the two pieces are being manufactured, temperature control is critical, and is carefully inspected.

Types of keel

Once the hull and deck have been assembled, there are various shapes of keel which may be fitted. It is, of course, essential for a sailing craft to have considerable ballast because of the thrust exercised on the sails and the consequent overbalancing or sideways drift which would result without underwater ballast. Basically the fin-keel and the twin bilge keel are the two alternatives. The fin-keel is fitted along the centre line of the craft and the twin bilge keels are fitted one on either side of the hull. The advantage of the latter is that the craft will have a shallower draft which, for many reasons (including the carriage of the boat on a trailer), is useful for the smaller family-type cruisers. However the performance of the fin-keeler, with its additional depth, is likely to be better.

Types of hull

Since a sailing vessel is seldom upright, the hull must be designed with this important point in mind. For this reason many of the out-and-out racers have a hull

33: A One Ton Cruiser/Racer depicts the typical style of hull design for the modern ocean racer

configuration with a considerable 'rounding' on the hull side. This is known as 'tumblehome'.

Multihulls

Not surprisingly, the multihulls, either catamaran or trimaran (with three hulls), are less likely to heel over. They do, however, have the disadvantage that they may 'flip' in unexpected conditions. If the sails are all 'sheeted in' and the craft is sailing hard on the wind, sudden increases in wind force can completely invert the boat. In large craft such as *British Oxygen* this is a real danger. One French boat has a hatch in the bottom of her main hull to enable the crew to escape if she does turn over.

The advantage of the 'catamaran' hull is, however, the enormous speed attainable. *British Oxygen*, a catamaran, and *Crossbow*, a mono-hull with outrigger, are two examples. Since the average fin-keel cruising boat has a normal maximum speed of around 10–11 knots, and the average cruising catamaran has more space and more speed, these craft (evolved, one might say, from craft designed by Polynesians!) have increased in popularity.

34 : The size of the man on board *British Oxygen* gives some indication of the vast beam of this craft

Chapter 7

SAFETY AT SEA

Signposts of the sea

In Great Britain the name of Grace Darling is well remembered by any who have studied history. A member of a family of eleven, she was trained by her father, a lighthouse keeper of the Longstone light. This is situated on the outermost main rock of the Farne Islands (5 miles from north Sunderland). In 1838 the *Forfarshire* struck the rocks and father and daughter set off from the light in a small fishing boat and rescued four men and a woman. A further four were then recovered. The whole adventure made the families who manned the lighthouses world-renowned for their lonely and arduous duties.

The Corporation of Trinity House, which is the organization for aids to navigation around the coasts of England, Wales and the Channel Islands, has a fascinating history. It stretches right back into the 'dark' Middle Ages. It is known to have had some

35: The Wolf Rock Lighthouse, Land's End. Comparatively recently this lonely lighthouse has been fitted with a helicopter platform for the delivery of supplies and the exchange of personnel

sort of an establishment at Deptford from a date before its incorporation by Henry VIII in 1514. By a charter granted by James II in 1685, during the lifetime of the ever-present Samuel Pepys (a one-time Master of the Trinity House), the powers and duties of the Corporation were laid down to include the compulsory pilotage of foreign ships in the River Thames and the licensing of pilots to guide them.

Previously, during the reign of Elizabeth I, the Corporation had been charged with the quite separate duty of setting up navigational marks. It was required to see to the provision of lighthouses and other navigational aids by setting up 'such and so many beacons, marks and signs in such place or places of the seashore and uplands near the seacoasts or forelands of the sea whereby the dangers may be avoided and escaped and ships the better come unto their ports without peril'.

There were privately owned lighthouses until 1836, when Trinity House was given powers to buy these from the owners. In such early days the power source of the lights included coal and oil wick burners, but nowadays many millions of candle-power are given out by these 'signposts'.

There are many lighthouses round the coasts of all countries and the design and pattern of these tend to be very similar. **36** depicts the Round House Lighthouse in the Scilly Isles, off the coast of Great Britain, which is typical of many such constructions all over the world.

One of the greatest dangers to mariners being fog, all lighthouses are equipped with varying sorts of machinery designed to give the strongest audible warning of a danger to navigation. The mournful note of the large 'diaphone' fog signal at the Round House Lighthouse, for example, is most comforting when it has been established that it is a long way away from the listening ship!

United States Coastguard

The United States Government, through the U.S. Coastguard Service, maintains more than 44,000 aids to mariners, about 300 of which are manned.

The first lighthouse in America was built in 1716 on the site of the latter-day Boston Light. As in other countries it was found necessary to set up proper lighthouses, rather than bonfires or blazing barrels of pitch, since shipwreckers merely duplicated these aids to lure the unwary mariner on to lonely stretches of coast where the ship might be plundered!

Boston also had one of the earliest fog signals, a loud cannon which was installed in 1719.

Apart from the provision of lighthouses, a lightship station was established at Craney Island in Hampton Roads, Virginia, in 1820. It consisted of a small decked-over boat.

It was not until 1789 that the U.S. Lighthouse Service was established as a government department.

Maintenance of lights

The U.S. Coastguards, in the same way as Trinity

36: The Round House Light-house in the Scilly Isles. Note the large 'dia-phone' fog sig-nalling equip-ment

House in the United Kingdom, have the onerous task of regularly inspecting the navigational aids. There are upwards of 24,000 buoys distributed along the inland and coastal waters of the United States which must be inspected for battery changing, removed for cleaning, repaired, reanchored and even replaced. For this purpose, and for lighthouse relief, the lighthouse authorities of the world maintain considerable numbers of large craft.

Trinity House Lighthouse Service

The British Trinity House Lighthouse Service vessel *Winston Churchill* sails many hundreds of sea miles in the course of a year on this sort of mission.

Characteristics of lighthouses

To the casual onlooker every lighthouse simply flashes a light, but every one has a separate and quite distinctive signal. It is this characteristic which makes the role of the lighthouse so indispensable to the mariner. There are eleven different characteristics which lighthouses may give to seaward. Some include a group of flashes at regular intervals; or a steady light which is eclipsed at regular intervals (known as an 'occulting' light); and some show different colours in succession on the same bearing.

Most lights have limited arcs of visibility and most are obscured on their landward side. Some have coloured sectors which warn mariners of local hazards (and also serve to tell the mariner, if he does not know already) *exactly* where he is.

He may take a bearing on a light when he is in the white 'sector' and as the light, to him, changes to red or green he will know exactly where he is in relation to the light, but, of course, not exactly how far off it he may be.

Apart from lighthouses, other signposts are light vessels, many of which are still in service. Light vessels are always red and usually have the name of the station in large white letters along the side of the hull. All light vessels have a prominent light tower and are equipped with powerful fog signalling equipment and a main navigation light.

38: When on station, each light vessel shows a characteristic light at night and in poor visibility. Due to high cost, such vessels are gradually being replaced by towers or large automatic buoys

Buoys and buoyage systems

All over the world the mariner approaching land requires buoyage 'signposts' and these are provided by the organizations which are members of the International Association of Lighthouse Authorities.

Two principal systems have been in use for many years. Round the United Kingdom the left-hand side of the main channel into a port or estuary is marked with red can-shaped buoys and the right-hand side of the main channel is marked with conical black buoys. There are, in addition, a number of other special buoys such as the horizontally striped middle-ground buoys which may be passed in safety, leaving them on either side of the vessel. This is the Lateral System.

The Cardinal System, used in most European countries, also consists of the use of can-shaped or conical buoys but they mark the danger by reference to the direction in which it lies. For example, if the mariner encounters a red and white horizontally striped can buoy, with a top mark of a cone pointing downwards, he will know that the danger lies to the north of such a mark.

The mariner can clearly distinguish between these two modes of buoyage, especially by using his charts. In certain places, however, the authorities use a mixture of both systems and it is possible to indicate this by special buoys. Certainly in European waters it will not be long before the two systems are combined.

For the enthusiast there are many books of reference which will explain all the details.

New aids to navigation

Nowadays the comparatively new Lanby buoy (the Large Automatic Navigational Buoy) has been used

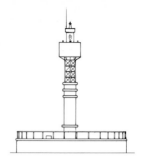

39: The Lanby, a large Automatic Navigational Buoy, anchored to the sea-bed. The light has a range of about 16 miles. The buoy is equipped with powerful fog-signalling equipment

in a number of places to replace the expensive, and man-power consuming, light vessels.

Light towers are also a comparatively new innovation. One of the first round the coasts of Britain was built at Newhaven, towed out to the position then occupied by the *Royal Sovereign* light vessel, and sunk on the sea bed. It is a large construction with helicopter pad and can be easily serviced.

40: The Light Tower at Royal Sovereign off the south coast of England which replaces a light-vessel. A well-known 'signpost' to mariners

Guardians of the mariner

In the United Kingdom Her Majesty's Coastguard today are largely concerned with the safety of navigation and the protection of life at sea. They were, however, originally formed to prevent smuggling and were part of H.M. Customs. Transferred to make better provision for defence, the protection of revenue and manning H.M. ships, the Coastguard remained part of the Admiralty until 1923.

As the principal co-ordinators of the Search and Rescue organization in Great Britain, the Coastguard liaise with the Royal National Life-boat Institution (with the assistance of Naval and Air Force helicopters) to form a very strong organization for the saving of life at sea. Other European countries have similar arrangements. In most cases the lifeboat service was set up in each country at the instigation of the public and is supported by public donation with, in some cases, additional aid from government funds.

Apart from the co-ordination duties of the British Coastguard, they have a large number of highly equipped operations rooms and look-out stations, together with a large mobile force equipped with cliff rescue apparatus. They also maintain a weather and and medical advice service for British trawlers operating far from their home ports.

In 1974 the British Royal National Life-boat

41 : *Miranda*, a special Department of Trade vessel, operated by H.M. Coastguard as a weather advisory and medical support ship for British trawlers

42: The British R.N.L.I. steel-hulled Waveney 44 at speed. Recently joined by the glass-reinforced plastic Arun 54, these craft give high-speed capability in all states of weather

Institution celebrated its 150th anniversary. The R.N.L.I. maintains a fleet of some 260 vessels ranging from the high-speed Arun 54 down to small inflatable craft for inshore work. The majority of the craft are self-righting.

The inshore lifeboats have been increased in number to assist, when closer inshore, all types of vessel, including an increasing number of pleasure craft. As in other countries the entire fleet is manned by volunteers and in one recent year about 3000 launches were made to answer emergency calls.

43: The British R.N.L.I. Atlantic 21 inshore lifeboat answering a 'Mayday' call at speed. The construction mounted on the stern is to assist the self-righting characteristics of the vessel in the event of capsize

On the continent of Europe the lifeboat service has developed from individual organizations. There were, at one time, in France four different organizations concerned with saving life at sea. Apart from governmental activities, the Société Nationale de Sauvetage en Mer now maintains over 260 stations and more than 440 craft of varying sizes.

In Holland the service was started in 1824. The coastline of Holland, in every westerly gale, was a wicked lee shore for sailing craft which were successfully plundered as soon as they were shipwrecked, not forgetting the enormous loss of life which was occasioned by the lack of assistance. Today the Koninklijke Noord-en Zuid-Hollandsche Redding-Maatschappij has a large fleet of sea-going lifeboats, beach lifeboats and other craft and remains a wholly voluntary organization supported by public subscription.

In the United States the U.S. Coastguard was created in 1790 with the construction of ten cutters for guarding against the activities of smugglers. The first cutter was the two-masted *Massachusetts*. For each cutter Congress authorized one master, not

44: The *Bernard van Leer*, one of the self-righting vessels operated by the Dutch (K.N.Z.H.R.M.) lifeboat service. She is stationed at Scheveningen and joined the fleet in 1965

45: The U.S. Coastguard was one of the first to use a helicopter capable of landing on the water. During this rescue the people were air-lifted to one of the Coastguard cutters, the *Diligence*

more than three mates, four mariners and two boys. (It is also recorded that the regular U.S. Navy was not organized until 1798.) There are now more than twenty-four distinct classes of ships and seven different types of aircraft in the service, dealing with everything from hunting down icebergs to the protection of seals; apart from the all-important function of protecting life at sea. At one point there were more than 170,000 men in the service.

46: The 378ft U.S. Coastguard cutter *Chase*. Her duties include long-range search and rescue, ocean patrol, oceanographic research and meteorology

Weather ships

One of the major duties of the large U.S. cutters is to serve as ocean station ships. They cruise for anything up to twenty-one days so that meteorologists can gather on-the-spot data to relay to the National Weather Service. At present the U.S. Coastguard maintains four stations in the Atlantic and two in the Pacific.

Other nations maintain surveillance in a similar fashion so that the mariner and, indeed, air traffic can be served both with weather information and rescue in the event of disaster.

Search and Rescue

In each country there are different arrangements about search and rescue but particularly in the crowded waters off the coasts of France and England a great network of organization stretches out to cover every possibility of loss of life at sea. The international liaison between European countries with a seaboard on the North Sea and English Channel is highly sophisticated, integrating as it does the lifeboat services, the Naval and Military aircraft and the official Coastguards whose duty it is to co-ordinate rescue sorties.

47: An operations room of the British Coastguard. Radar surveillance of the traffic in crowded waters is a 24-hour operation

Navigation lights on vessels

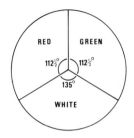

48: The 'sectors' of a sailing vessel's navigation lights. If these are properly screened an observer can tell (at night) in which direction another vessel is travelling

RED GREEN

112½°   112½°

135°

WHITE

Every vessel which sails the seas at night is identifiable by its navigation lights. To take the simplest set of lights (those of a sailing vessel under sail only), there will be a green light on her starboard side (the right-hand side looking forward); a red light on her port side (again looking from the stern towards the bows) and a white light which 'faces' astern, to warn overtaking craft that she is there. These lights, as are all other navigation lights, are 'screened' so that they only show over a defined and internationally agreed sector. Hence, if you were in a vessel which is overtaking a sailing vessel, you would first see a white stern light fairly low down on the sailing vessel. As you, for example, overtake on her right-hand side (passing up her starboard side and leaving her to your port side) the white stern light would eventually disappear and you would see her green starboard light. If she were sailing across your bows, showing you her starboard side, you would see her green light for a long time until she had 'turned her tail' on you, when her white stern light would appear.

'Rules of the road' at sea

For reasons of space it is impossible to include all the details of the steering and sailing rules—which would require a whole book in themselves—and, indeed, all the information on how to identify a craft by her lights, but it is hoped that the little we have been able to give on these subjects will add interest to even the shortest journey by sea and explain what is going on when two vessels are approaching each other.

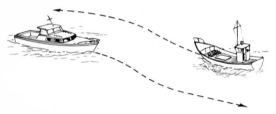

49: 'When two powered craft are meeting end on or nearly end on so as to involve risk of collision each shall alter course to starboard'

Within the International Regulations for Preventing Collisions at Sea, a universally agreed code of conduct, there are also rules about what two vessels should do when close to each other and steering different courses which might result in collision. At its simplest, when two powered craft are going straight towards each other, they turn to starboard (right) and pass each other, showing their port (left) sides. Imagine a narrow channel with two craft approaching each other. It is the same as a road in a country in which the cars are driven on the right of the road. For most countries it is easy to understand the rule of the road at sea, at least when approaching each other from opposite directions.

Imagine two powered craft approaching each other at right angles and at considerable speed. Their combined speeds could be anything around 35 m.p.h. The captains must avoid collision and the rules made internationally and understood by every mariner provide an immediate answer. The captain who sees the other ship on his starboard side is the one whose primary duty it is to avoid collision. The other captain also has a duty to avoid collision but he has the priority—he is the 'stand on vessel'. He will only take avoiding action when he is absolutely certain that, for some reason, the 'give-way vessel' is going to fail to do so.

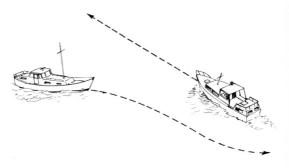

50: When two power-driven vessels are crossing so as to involve risk of collision, the vessel which has the other on her starboard side shall keep out of the way of the other

Except in very exceptional circumstances, a power-driven vessel must keep out of the way of a sailing vessel because it is clearly easier for a powered craft to alter course and get well clear of a possible collision. However, in narrow channels the sailing vessel must leave room for a large ship.

The rules about sailing vessels meeting each other

depend upon a decision as to which tack a vessel is on. If the wind is coming on to the right-hand side of a sailing vessel she is said to be on starboard tack and has priority over a vessel with the wind on her port side.

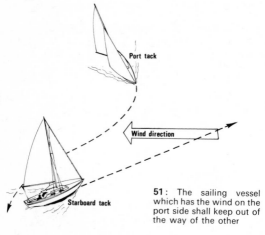

Port tack

Wind direction

Starboard tack

51: The sailing vessel which has the wind on the port side shall keep out of the way of the other

If both vessels are on the same tack then the vessel which is to windward shall keep out of the way of the other.

And finally every vessel, whether power or sail, which is overtaking another has a duty to keep clear. This is clearly sound commonsense since the captain of the vessel being overtaken may have his back to the overtaking vessel!

Of course there are many more rules than these few but they are the principal ones which will explain the majority of manœuvres when ships are at close quarters.

Signalling

Ever since fleets of craft have sailed in company it has been necessary to communicate with each other and necessary to distinguish friend from foe. Prior to the advent of radio, or Morse code and lights, such communication was done by flags, and the practice is still carried out today.

Ships of all nations, whether commercial or private, under power or sail, distinguish themselves by wearing the maritime flag of their nation at or near the stern of the vessel. The British maritime ensigns are the Red, the White and the Blue Ensign originally worn to distinguish parts of the same fleet and their Admirals. Other nations wear the maritime flag and many of these are depicted on Plate 8. When a vessel enters the territorial waters of another nation it will also wear the ensign of that nation superior to the position of its own ensign. Hence a vessel with a French flag at the stern and the British Red Ensign somewhere aloft is a French vessel in British territorial waters.

Every vessel is equipped with a set of flags for each letter of the alphabet. These are internationally agreed and are depicted on Plate 1. Each flag also has a single meaning. These are as follows:

A —I have a diver down; keep well clear at slow speed.
B —I am taking in, or discharging, or carrying dangerous goods.
C —Yes.
D —Keep clear of me; I am manœuvring with difficulty.
E —I am altering my course to starboard.
F —I am disabled; communicate with me.
G —I require a pilot.
H —I have a pilot on board.
I —I am altering my course to port.

J —I am on fire and have dangerous cargo on board; keep well clear of me.
K —I wish to communicate with you.
L —You should stop your vessel instantly.
M—My vessel is stopped and making no way through the water.
N —No.
O —Man overboard.
P —*In Harbour*. All persons should report on board as the vessel is about to put to sea.
   At Sea. Flag P may be used by fishing vessels to mean 'my nets have come fast on an obstruction'.
Q—My vessel is healthy and I request free pratique.
(R—No signal has been allocated.)
S —My engines are going astern.
T —Keep clear of me; I am engaged in pair trawling.
U —You are running into danger.
V —I require assistance.
W—I require medical assistance.
X —Stop carrying out your intentions and watch for my signals.
Y —I am dragging my anchor.
Z —I require a tug.

Some of these letters have special secondary meanings in particular circumstances, but it will be noted that they are mostly urgent signals.

The letters of the alphabet may, of course, be used to spell out words, but this is slow and laborious. The International Code contains groups of letters which are assigned special whole-message meanings to save time. Messages which are likely to be needed by all mariners such as distress, casualties, damage, navigation, manœuvres, meteorology, communications, pratique and medical, are covered by two- or three-letter hoists. For example, QL means 'You should go astern'.

Clearly these flag signals and the use of hand-held semaphore flags are useful only in daylight. At night, over short distances, the Morse code is sent by light. Nowadays, with the increasing use of radio and radio-telephony, the various laborious flag signalling methods are less used but still essential.

Sailing boats and their 'signals'

Because the majority of sailing craft are now being used for pleasure, there are numerous codes of practice which have sprung up over the years. Again, these are all based upon the practice of mariners in the past. Apart from the International Code of Signals, the flags and ensigns commonly flown from or worn by yachts fall into several categories. The ensign or maritime flag of a nation has already been discussed. Some yacht clubs have their own ensign.

The Club burgee or special flag of officers

Most yacht clubs have a distinctive burgee which is the correct description for a triangular flag. This is flown from the main masthead. The Commodore, Vice-Commodore and Rear Commodore have distinctive flags of the same design but of different shape. The Commodore flies a broad pennant, usually swallow-tailed, the Vice-Commodore the same but with one ball in the upper left quarter of the pennant. The Rear Commodore's pennant is distinguished by two balls. These vary in position from club to club. That depicted on Plate 1 is perhaps unusual. Other clubs have the two balls vertical, either both in the upper left quarter (canton) of the pennant, or one in the upper and one in the lower quarter nearest the mast. The tendency is to follow Naval custom and, therefore, customs vary from country to country. What has been described here is the custom in the United Kingdom. Where a club wishes to honour a Past Commodore or President,

Admiral or Patron, he may sometimes fly a rectangular flag bearing the club's emblem or design.

House flags

All shipping companies have a private flag which, when flown from a ship, denotes the company to which that ship belongs. Equally yachtsmen are 'entitled' to design their own distinguishing flag which, more often than not, they use as their racing flag. These are usually rectangular in shape and are flown in place of the club burgee. Thus a yacht which is racing is immediately distinguishable from one which is not. Also it is common practice for yachts racing to strike the ensign, if they are large enough to wear one, while they are racing. These two actions—the wearing of a rectangular masthead flag and the absence of an ensign—are sure signs to another craft that the vessel in question is racing.

Dressing overall and saluting

The observer may on occasion see a vessel bedecked with the complete set of International Code Flags. This is known as 'dressing overall' and is carried out on occasions such as national festivals, for local regattas, Royal birthdays, the arrival of Royalty or dignitaries at a port or at launching ceremonies. The flags of the International Code are strung from stem-head to masthead, from masthead to masthead, when the craft has more than one mast, and down to the stern. Additionally craft with a bowsprit may continue the flags down to water level below the sprit.

Saluting other craft follows Naval practice. Salutes are made by 'dipping' the ensign or maritime flag. It is lowered to a position about one-third from the end of its hoist. The ship being saluted will do the same and then re-hoist. The ship making the salute will keep her ensign at the 'dip' until the ship being saluted starts to re-hoist her ensign.

Chapter 8

SAILING CRUISERS AND OFFSHORE RACERS

In a book of this length it would be quite impossible to depict all the craft which may be seen in the modern recreational and professional small craft world. There are, however, three major categories into which those chosen for inclusion may be divided.

In this chapter is a selection of varying sizes of sailing pleasure craft used for racing and cruising and which have varying sizes of accommodation below. They range from 5·18m (17ft) to 21·64m (71ft) in overall length, and from the smallest cruiser to the fastest racing craft. There are many reasons for the selection. In some cases the quantity which is sailing makes them of interest; in other cases, the speciality of their design and again their success in racing.

In Chapter 9 (Dayboats), open craft, with no real overnight accommodation, have been selected for much the same reasons. There are many which have been granted International status because of their world-wide popularity; there are some which, although world-wide have been granted only National status by one country and there are others which are typical of the type of craft which will be seen all over the world in pure cruising or training situations.

Almost invariably the observer will be surprised at the arrival of many identical craft at a particular place within a short space of time. This is, of course, because some club has provided racing facilities and the craft tend to race as one class. On other occasions, a selection of various types will patently be aiming for the same spot. This will undoubtedly be a 'menagerie' dinghy class run by a club or larger vessels racing under handicap rules of some kind, or perhaps a sailing school.

In many countries there will be 'regional' classes which are seldom seen elsewhere. Equally there will be a variety of use including lake sailing, inland waterway cruising in powerboats and sailing boats, inshore open boat sailing and the sterner stuff of offshore cruising and racing.

While you are observing the scene you may at times think that the whole sport looks rather dangerous, but this is only because to the uninitiated a vessel which is heeled over does appear to be in trouble. The majority of the craft discussed in this book are, however, specifically designed to remain buoyant and afloat when capsized. This is particularly true of the boats included in the dayboat section. Most countries have standards of construction to which the recognized builders adhere. Although a rowing boat may tend to sink when swamped, the majority of sailing dayboats most certainly will not, being constructed with considerable buoyancy in water-tight tanks either in the stern, the bow or 'seats' of the craft or by the provision of buoyancy bags which are secured into the craft.

With regard to powerboat safety, the larger craft are well equipped with pumps and most of the smaller ones have just sufficient buoyancy to support their heavy engines if by chance they capsize.

The selection contained in the powerboat section (Chapter 10) is designed to illustrate the main types of craft, it being impossible to include all that is available.

Nevertheless, it is hoped that the observer will, at least, be able to identify the majority of craft (with the aid of sail insignia or particular characteristics) and find them in these pages.

52: Alacrity 22/670		**53: Arpège**	
L.O.A.	6·66m (21ft 10in)	L.O.A.	9·25m (30ft 4in)
Beam	2·34m (7ft 8in)	Beam	3·00m (9ft 10in)
Draft (keel down)1·53m (5ft)		Draft 1·35m (4ft 5in)	

Variously known as the **Alacrity 22,** Catalina 22 or Jaguar 22, depending upon the place of manufacture, this craft, weighing around 850kg (16¾cwt) is very light in comparison with other craft of similar length. This and her movable keel make her ideal for trailer sailing. She was designed by Frank Butler with the American market well in mind. She has a large cockpit with a wide hatchway leading below.

The French company, Michel Dufour Société Anonyme, was set up in 1964 and its really successful design, the **Arpège**, was presented at the Paris Boat Show in 1967. The company has produced many successful designs which are discussed in this book. The underwater configuration of the Arpège, with its bulb keel, is relatively unusual in a cruising or racing craft. These variations in design below the waterline, although not often seen by the observer, make a considerable difference to the performance of craft.

65

54: Atlanta/Hurley 24   55: Atlanta 8·5

L.O.A.	7·34m (24ft 1in)	L.O.A.	8·5m (28ft)
Beam	2·26m (7ft 5in)	Beam	2·79m (9ft 2in)
Draft (fin keel)	1·24m (4ft 1in)	Draft	1·16m (3ft 10in)
(bilge keel)	1·20m (3ft 11in)		

Designed by I.L. Anderson, the **Atlanta/Hurley 24** can be used for everything from early cruising training to extended passage-making in very adverse conditions. A small cruiser, with tiller steering, she is easily handled even in the most extreme weather and has the reputation of being a very 'dry' boat to sail, the cockpit being well protected by a moderately high coachroof.

Atlanta 8·5 is from an original design by C.J.S. Roy. A twin-keeler, she has been used for Trans-Atlantic crossing making 123 miles per day and travels well at 6 knots which, for a craft of this size, is very adequate. When under the 10 h.p. Bukh engine she was reported as being extremely quiet.

56: Atlanta 29 Motor Sailer   **57: Atlanta 32**

L.O.A. 8·68m (28ft 6in)	L.O.A. 9·75m (32ft)
Beam 3·04m (10ft)	Beam 3·05m (10ft)
Draft 1·21m (4ft)	Draft 1·22m (4ft)
	Engine Mercedes OM636
	Mk II 42hp diesel.

Chosen for its motor-sailer look, the **Atlanta 29** was designed by G.L. Watson architects, famous for their fishing vessels and lifeboats. With the sturdy and well-known Mercedes OM 636 4-cylinder 42 h.p. marine diesel engine this craft is a real 50/50 motor sailer.

A similar design (the **32**) by J.A. Bennett and Associates is marketed by the same company. The length/beam ratio provides an exceptionally roomy boat and her ketch rig provides reasonably small sails to be handled by the family. The aft-cabin version with a centre cockpit sleeps seven on board, displaces 7 tons, and is a fine example of a well-protected sea-going family craft.

58: Ballad

L.O.A. 9·14m (30ft)
Beam 2·96m (9ft 9in)
Draft 1·55m (5ft 1in)

59: Bowman 36

L.O.A. 10·97m (36ft)
Beam 3·45m (11ft 4in)
Draft 1·68m (5ft 6in)

Constructed by Albin Marin AB of Kristinehamn, Sweden, and designed by Rolf Magnusson, the Albin **Ballad** is an ocean racer in the Half Ton Class. She is fitted with internal halyards running back to the cockpit. She is a development from an earlier design, the Joker, and has been successfully raced in many world events. In the first three years after introduction more than 900 of these craft were sold.

Bowman 36, twice winner of the Silver and Gold Award at the London Boat Show, was designed by Holman and Pye. This craft can be rigged as a ketch or sloop. She carries a Mercedes-Benz Diesel OM 636 very nearly amidships on the port side. This unusual position provides easy access to this powerful engine. Another unusual feature is that she may be equipped with a retractable centreboard instead of the conventional fin-keel.

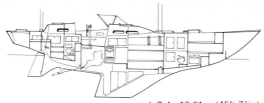

60: Bowman 46

L.O.A. 13·91m (45ft 7½in)
Beam 3·4m (12ft 11in)
Draft 2·1m (7ft)

As the line drawing of the interior shows, the **Bowman 46** is yawl rigged with a centre cockpit, providing room for an after cabin. The Bowman Corsair may be yawl or sloop rigged and has approximately the same overall hull dimensions. The largest vessel of this marque is the Bowman 57 with berths on board for twelve.

61: Carbineer 46

L.O.A. 14·17m (46ft 6in)
Beam 3·72m (12ft 2in)
Draft 1·83m (6ft)

Typical of the large motor-sailer, the **Carbineer 46,** designed by Laurent Giles and Partners, is powered by a 6-cylinder Perkins 6·35 diesel engine and she is ketch rigged which provides perhaps the easiest rig for a cruising crew to handle. The vessel is built to a very high standard for ocean work.

62: Carter 30

L.O.A.	9·07m	(29ft 9in)
Beam	3·10m	(10ft 1in)
Draft	1·68m	(5ft 6in)

The **Carter 30** was designed by Dick Carter for the Half Ton Cup racing enthusiast. The hull has a fine 'entry' and a flattish underwater shape, with a high aspect ratio fin keel. She carries her rudder as far aft as possible on a deep skeg and the propeller of the Yanmar YS 12 diesel is set almost amidships. The underwater profile is a departure from the conventional, and the craft in her first races achieved considerable success.

63: Carter 3/4 Tonner

L.O.A.	9·98m	(32ft 9in)
Beam	3·4m	(11ft 1½in)
Draft	1·82m	(6ft)

This craft is designed to win the Three-Quarter Ton Cup and the overall length is kept down. She has a deep upright rudder and skeg set as far aft as possible. 'Peticache', the standard production boat, acted as a prototype and, having won a trophy for the Top Production boat in a World Championship, has been slightly modified for the production boats. She was designed by Dick Carter.

64: Centurion

L.O.A.	9·75m (32ft)
Beam	3·00m (9ft 10in)
Draft	1·78m (5ft 10in)

65: Comet

L.O.A.	9·10m (30ft)
Beam (max)	3·06m (10ft)
Draft	1·40m (4ft 6in)
Draft (max—optional)	1·70m (5ft 6in)

Designed by the well-known Holman and Pye, the **Centurion** typifies the comfortable cruising yacht. French-built, British-designed, she rates under Class V of the International Offshore Rating Rule for racing craft. With a longer mast and larger sail area she comes into Class IV. She has the now characteristic uncluttered cockpit so important for efficient racing.

A combined design by E.G. van de Stadt and the Group Finot, **Comet** is the winner of many famous races in numerous countries. With a fine tapered stem and a high free-board, she also has the advantage of a large and well-designed cockpit from which most of the work can be done. Despite her somewhat unconventional look she carries the 'imprint' of two famous designers.

66: Contessa 26

L.O.A. 7·77m (25ft 6in)
Beam   2·28m (7ft 6in)
Draft   1·21m (4ft)

67: Contessa 32

L.O.A. 9·92m (32ft)
Beam   2·98m (9ft 6in)
Draft   1·74m (5ft 6in)

The **Contessa 32** was the top award-winner at the 1972 London Boat Show. She was developed from the very successful **Contessa 26** which was also designed by David Sadler. The larger craft has 6 berths and is fitted out to the highest standards. The ancillary equipment, so important for ease of operation, includes Lewmar winches (which are world-renowned for their quality and strength) and the Volvo Penta 2-cylinder petrol engine.

The larger **Contessa 35,** designed by Peterson, has established an enviable reputation in the One Ton Cup races, where there are numerous examples of this out-and-out racer.

68: Coronado 25

L.O.A. 7·60m (25ft)
Beam 2·44m (8ft)
Draft 1·10m (3ft 11in)

Coronado 35

L.O.A. 10·60m (34ft 8in)
Beam 3·07m (10ft 1in)
Draft 1·14m (3ft 9in)

Over 2000 **Coronado 25s** are sailing throughout the world. Designed by F. Butler and built by Playvisa in Spain, she races in Class VI under the rules of the International Offshore Rating Council. With tiller steering, the 25 can be fitted with inboard or outboard engine. As will be seen from the illustration, there are no side-decks so the crew gains access to the foredeck 'over the top'.

Coronado 35 (not illustrated) is also American designed and built in Spain. She has a large cabin aft which can be reached under cover beneath the cockpit. She is extremely spacious with good headroom and a relatively broad beam. She stands very high out of the water which enhances the space below. For this reason she has a high ballast ratio, but even so, a considerable sail area for her size.

69: Dufour 27

L.O.A.	8·30m	(27ft 3in)
Beam	2·79m	(9ft 2in)
Draft	1·58m	(5ft 2in)

70: Dufour 31

L.O.A.	9·40m	(30ft 7in)
Beam	3·20m	(10ft 6in)
Draft	1·74m	(5ft 9in)

To the observer (at a distance) there are only slight differences in this range of the Group Finot designs built by Michel Dufour S.A. The 24, 27, 31 and 34 are all very similar in exterior appearance, the hull design being only very slightly different. The difference in the various craft in the range lies, of course, in the performance and accommodation provided by the various sizes.

In the illustrations of the **27** and the **31** notice the slight difference in the shape of the bows and also the 'taller' coachroof of the 31.

The company is responsible for a number of other very successful designs.

72: Écume FD *(above)*

A flush-decked version of the Écume de Mer specially built for racing

71: Écume de Mer

L.O.A.	8·00m	(26ft 3in)
Beam	2·70m	(8ft 8in)
Draft (cruising version)	1·25m	(4ft 1in)
(racing version)	1·50m	(5ft)

Built by Chantiers Mallard of La Rochelle, Perigny, France, to a design of the J.M. Finot Group, the **Écume de Mer** is an 8m (26¼ft), high performance racing craft. First introduced in 1970, there were more than 750 sailing by the end of 1974. The craft is the winner of many international events including the U.S. Quarter Ton Cup and twice winner of the European equivalent. As a cruising boat she has been highly praised, particularly for cockpit comfort and safety features.

The **Écume FD,** which is a racing version of the same design, has been constructed with a completely flush deck, which makes for easier working when racing. This radically alters the silhouette of the craft and provides less headroom below. This aspect is, of course, of little consequence in an out-and-out racer.

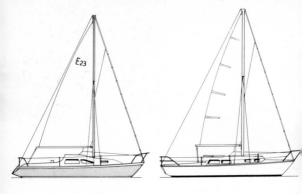

**73: Elizabethan
23 Mk II**

L.O.A.	6·9m	(23ft)	
Beam	2·2m	(7ft	1in)
Draft (plate up)	0·7m	(2ft	6in)
(plate down)	1·3m	(4ft	11in)

L.O.A.	10·40m	(33ft)	**74: Elizabethan**
Beam	2·80m	(9ft 4in)	**33 sloop**
Draft	1·2m	(4ft 7in)	

The smallest in the range of successful 'Elizabethans', the **23** has a retractable centreplate. A specially raised coachroof provides headroom of 1·7m (5ft 6in).

The Elizabethan 30 (originally known as the Elizabethan 9 metre) hit the headlines when she was the winner of the Island Sailing Club's Gold Cup in the Round the Island Race, an annual event round the Isle of Wight which attracts probably the largest single fleet of yachts of all shapes and sizes. A David Thomas design, she has continued to be a successful seller. The hull was designed after considerable tank testing, particular attention being given to the development of the skeg and rudder.

The **Elizabethan 33** is available in three stages of completion to minimize initial costs.

75: Fleur de Mer

L.O.A.	9·60m	(31ft)
Beam	3·35m	(10ft 11in)
Draft	1·50m–1·70m	(5ft–5ft 7in)

76: Halcyon 23
(above)

L.O.A.	7·01m	(23ft)
Beam	2·28m	(7ft 6in)
Draft (fin keel)	1·12m	(3ft 8in)
(bilge keel)	0·76m	(2ft 6in)

Created by the Group Finot, **Fleur de Mer** was designed primarily for fast cruising. The deck is free of 'clutter' and the whole layout gives ease of handling. She has a large cockpit, with the main-sheet track placed on the coachroof which leaves the cockpit clear for the crew to work in safety. She is a successor to the Écume de Mer and Rêve de Mer, both successful designs. Besides inbuilt strength, the main bulkheads are of marine plywood, bonded and bolted into the ribbing of the hull. The coach-roof has a removable cover protecting all the halyards which run back to the cockpit.

Halcyon 23 craft, designed by Alan Buchanan, are now sailing in the Baltic, Mediterranean, and United Kingdom waters and on the American and Canadian seaboards. The Halcyon 23 is an economical, fast and enjoyable boat to use. The auxiliary engine is a 7 h.p. Wickstrom 4-stroke single-cylinder petrol engine.

77: Halcyon 27

L.O.A.	8·23m (27ft)
Beam	2·34m (7ft 8in)
Draft	1·22m (4ft)

78: High Tension 36

L.O.A.	10·86m (35ft 9in)
Beam	3·55m (11ft 8in)
Draft	2·05m (6ft 9in)

The **Halcyon 27,** also designed by Alan Buchanan, is a distinguished high-performance cruising yacht with a long keel which gives considerable stability in a seaway. Fitted with a petrol or optional diesel engine, she makes all of 6 knots under engine. The deck, cabin top and cockpit is a one-piece moulding of 'foam sandwich' construction which provides considerable rigidity.

Designed by Jac de Ridder **High Tension** is built by Southern Ocean Shipyard Ltd of Great Britain. This craft was put into production after its successful showing in the British One Ton Cup event in 1974. Underwater, her aft sections are flat, like many a dinghy, designed to lift out of the water and to 'plane' at high speeds.

79: Hustler 25·5

L.O.A.	7·77m	(25ft 6in)
Beam	2·65m	(8ft 8½in)
Draft	1·47m	(4ft 10in)

80: Hustler 30

L.O.A.	9·15m	(30ft)
Beam	2·79m	(9ft 2in)
Draft	1·67m	(5ft 6in)

While the range of Hustlers have made a name for themselves in the British East Anglian Offshore racing circuit, they have taken honours in Holland, in the Half Ton Cup series, and the **30** has been raced in the Fastnet race. All designed by the partnership of Holman and Pye, there is a size to suit every need. The **25·5** is typical of the fast cruiser for a crew of three, and the **30** and **35** (page 80) with skeg-hung rudder and deep fin-keel are clearly designed to sail fast and have also achieved considerable success in the Middle Sea Channel and Dinard Races. Anything over 200 miles long, such races test crew and craft to the full.

81: Hustler 35

L.O.A.	10·67m	(35ft)
Beam	3·17m	(10ft 7in)
Draft	1·83m	(6ft)

For the observer, there are a number of points to note in illustrations **79** and **80**. In **79,** the **Hustler 25·5** (page 79) is carrying the insignia of Class IV which assists the race officers managing a number of fleets to identify in which fleet a craft is sailing. She also, it should be noted, is not carrying an ensign. This is another sign that she is racing. In case of retirement, it is the accepted practice to lower the racing flag from the masthead and to fly the burgee (a triangular pennant) and to wear the Ensign.

In **80** (page 79) the concern being shown by the crew is to ensure that the spinnaker is setting correctly. Particularly in light airs, it is extremely difficult to ensure that the spinnaker remains filled.

82: Jouet 27 (Tarantelle)

L.O.A.   8·00m   (26ft 5in)
Beam   2·88m   (9ft 5in)
Draft   1·55m   (4ft 11in)

83: Kingfisher 20 plus

L.O.A.   6·58m   (21ft 7in)
Beam   2·1m   (6ft 11in)
Draft   0·70m   (2ft 4in)

Jouet 27 (Tarantelle) is a five-berth cruiser/racer, (designed by Philip Harlé) which, under the racing rules, is in Class V or VI depending on engine and rig. She is round-bilged with a deep fin. She is extensively raced in French and British waters and has had many successes in such races and in Junior Offshore Group races and the International La Rochelle Week. Typical of the modern smaller racing vessels, she is not a 'stripped out' racing machine but is a comfortable cruising boat with a number of clever space-saving features in the interior design.

A twin-keel Bermudan sloop designed by R.A.G. Nierop, the **Kingfisher 20 +** is a good example of the small cruiser with some interesting design features not the least of which is the ingenious outboard mounting. The motor is permanently fixed in a locker aft of the cockpit and, when required, the shaft is turned down through an opening in the hull. A Chinese junk rig is an interesting variant.

84: Kingfisher 26

L.O.A. 7·92m (26ft)
Beam 2·33m (7ft 8in)
Draft 1·00m (3ft 2in)

Designed by R.A.G. Nierop, this family cruising boat obtained excellent reviews for the practical interior layout and her ability (despite her shallow draft) to remain well balanced when under a press of sail. One of the class won the Mono-Hull Handicap Trophy in the single-handed Transatlantic race in 1972. She is easily distinguished by an unusually long and high coachroof.

The Kingfisher 30, by the same designer, has an after cabin incorporated into the design which is visible in the illustration of the **30 S.**

85: Kingfisher 30 S

L.O.A. 9·1m (30ft)
Beam 2·74m (9ft)
Draft 1·19m (3ft 11in)

Leisure 17 (not illustrated)

L.O.A.	5·18m	(17ft)
Beam	2·13m	(7ft)
Draft (twin keel)	0·65m	(2ft 2in)
(fin keel)	0·97m	(3ft 2in)

			86: Leisure 22
L.O.A.	6·71m	(22ft)	*(above)*
Beam	2·39m	(7ft 10in)	
Draft (twin keel)	0·81m	(2ft 8in)	
(fin keel)	1·19m	(3ft 11½in)	

Designed by Arthur Howard and built by Cobra-
mold of Essex, England, the Leisure 17 has won a
reputation for being perfectly balanced and con-
trollable. Clearly a craft of this size should not be
used for extended open sea passages but she is ideally
suited for inshore work. Headroom below is, as might
be expected, only 1·2m (4ft) which would restrict
her use for long periods of time. Her 'sister ship' the
Leisure 20 was designed by Horst E. Glacer of
Bremen.

The **Leisure 22,** designed by Graham Caddick,
presents a somewhat similar profile and provides that
little extra headroom and space to make her a comfortable small family cruiser. As will be seen from
illustration **86,** she has a pleasing line.

88: Macwester 27 Series II

L.O.A.	8·20m	(27ft)
Beam	2·76m	(9ft 2in)
Draft	1·12m	(3ft 8in)

87: Macwester Rowan 22

L.O.A.	6·8m	(22ft 3in)
Beam	2·5m	(8ft 3in)
Draft	0·83m	(2ft 9in)

With an inboard 5 h.p. Stuart Turner engine and a hinged mast step for easy lowering, the **Rowan 22** is very suitable for inland waterways but nevertheless has achieved any number of long sea voyages. Extensively used by a well-known British charter firm, she is highly regarded. With a displacement of 4 tons (Thames Measurement), she is supplied with many variations and can be fitted with diesel or petrol inboard engines, or with an outboard engine, according to choice. C.S.J. Roy designed the Rowan 22, and also the **Macwester 27 Series II** which was extensively tank tested by the University of Southampton. A twin-keeled yacht of good performance, she is typical of the craft and the quality expected of this company.

89: Marcon Cutlass 27 Mk II

L.O.A. 8·23m (27ft)
Beam 2·33m (7ft 8in)
Draft 1·37m (4ft 6in)

This classic long-keeled craft is a cruiser/racer and, with the modified deck layout of the **Mark III** version, has achieved some considerable racing successes at the Scottish Clyde Week, the Round Gotland Baltic race and various lesser regattas. She has been sailed on many long-distance cruises and made numerous Atlantic crossings. For those who wish it, she can be purchased for individual interior fitting-out. A petrol or diesel 10 h.p. auxiliary engine is the recommended power unit.

Marcon Rival 32 (not illustrated) also lends itself to a variety of individual interior designs. With a sail area, under mainsail and genoa, of 38·2m² (411ft²) she is ideal for long-distance cruising. Designed by Peter Brett, she has made some successful ocean trips of around 7000–9000 miles. She is rated for ocean racing at about 22·7ft (there are a number of special measurements applied to all racing yachts which bring them to a 'handicap' figure). At this rating, she has competed successfully.

90: Morgan IOR 36 T   91: Nantucket Clipper

L.O.A.	10·89m (35ft 9in)		L.O.A.	9·65m (31ft 8in)
Beam	3·58m (11ft 9in)		Beam	2·78m (9ft 1½in)
Draft (approx)	1·9m (6ft 3in)		Draft	1·30m (4ft 3in)

Big brother of the Morgan fleet from the Morgan Yacht Corporation of Florida, U.S.A., the **Morgan IOR 36 T** comes from a long line of race-winning craft. She has a somewhat unusual T-shaped cockpit and, for cruising, is powered by a 30 h.p. V-drive engine. The smaller yachts in the range have chalked up successes: the Morgan IOR 33 T in the North American Yacht Racing Union's Three-Quarter Ton National Championship, and the Morgan 27 in the MORC National Championship.

Designed by Alan Buchanan, with a high ballast ratio and a wide beam, the **Nantucket Clipper** is a lively cruising craft, with a small marine diesel unit as standard equipment. The distinctive fine-entry clipper bow is the distinguishing feature of the craft and lends character.

92: Nautor 50 Motor-sailer

L.O.A.   15·1m (49ft 7in)
Beam   4·6m (15ft 1in)
Draft   1·7m (5ft 7in)

L.O.A.   9·98m (32ft 9in)
Beam   3·05m (10ft)
Draft   1·22m (4ft)

93: Neptune and Neptunian

Designed by Sparkman and Stephens and constructed by Nautor of Finland, the **Nautor 50** is a
departure from the whole range of Swan craft
designed and built by this team. Powered with a
Perkins 6-cylinder marine diesel engine, the Nautor is
intended to be the ultimate in large motor-sailers.

Designed by Alan Buchanan and partners, the
Neptune with its aft cockpit and the **Neptunian**
(illustrated) with its centre cockpit fully justify the
title of 'motor-sailer'. Powered by a Perkins diesel,
they can average between 7 and 8 knots under
power alone. Both have a considerable 'spread of
canvas' with 51m² (549ft²) in the main and genoa.
The Neptunian carries a mizzen of 7m² (75ft²).

94: Nicholson 30 Mk II

L.O.A.	8·8m	(28ft 11in)
Beam	2·97m	(9ft 9½in)
Draft	1·73m	(5ft 7¼in)

95: Nicholson 32 Mk X

L.O.A.	10·05m	(33ft)
Beam	2·81m	(9ft 3in)
Draft	1·68m	(5ft 6in)

At the lower end of the range of world-famous Nicholson yachts, built by Camper and Nicholsons Ltd, is the **Nicholson 30,** designed as a Half Ton Cup boat. She has achieved considerable success on the racing circuit, being the fastest Half Tonner in Britain in 1974, and fifth in the World Championships in 1974 at La Rochelle. The Mark II has a displacement of 3·25 tons in comparison to the Nicholson 55—which displaces 17 tons.

The **Nicholson 32** is perhaps the best known of the range, since it set something of a pattern as long ago as 1964 for a production cruising boat. More than 300 have been built and the vessel has achieved international fame.

96: Nicholson 35

L.O.A.   10·74m (35ft 11in)
Beam   3·18m (10ft 5in)
Draft   1·68m (5ft 6in)

The **Nicholson 35** is a very popular size within the whole range of Nicholson boats. She displaces 7 tons and is a comfortable cruising yacht with the usual high standard of accommodation expected from this firm.

The **Nicholson 42** was a winner of the London International Boat Show Award in 1974. She is built with either ketch or sloop rig. The company recognizes the importance of paying particular attention to clever internal design, so necessary on every yacht for the comfort of the crew. Note the underwater profile which is fairly typical of the Nicholson range.

97: Nicholson 42

L.O.A.   12·75m (41ft 10in)
Beam   3·72m (12ft 2½in)
Draft   1·68m (5ft 6in)

98: Nicholson 48

L.O.A. 14·53m (47ft 8in)
Beam   3·94m (12ft 11in)
Draft   1·68m (5ft 6in)

(below)

99: Nicholson 55

L.O.A. 16·57m (54ft 5in)
Beam   4·37m (14ft 4in)
Draft   2·51m (8ft 3in)

The **48** is a cruising ketch and is a long-distance cruiser with good accommodation for seven people in four separate cabins. This craft has proved particularly popular in the Mediterranean and on the Eastern seaboard of the United States.

The **Nicholson 55,** normally built as a centre cockpit cruising boat, was raced, in an after-cockpit version, in the 1973 Admiral's Cup representing the United Kingdom. **Quailo** (illustrated) represented the United Kingdom in the Southern Cross Series in January 1974. Numerous 55s have been bought for Service sailing. The British Joint Services Sailing Centre (at Gosport, England) is a model of co-operation between Army, Navy and Air Force.

100: Nicholson 33

Waterline length	8·4m	(27ft 7in)
Beam	3·17m	(10ft 1in)

101: Norlin 34

L.O.A.	10·48m	(34ft 5in)
Beam	3·37m	(11ft 1in)
Draft	1·82m	(6ft)

With the preoccupation, in recent years, over Quarter, Half, Three-Quarter and One Ton Cup racing, it is hardly surprising that a number of manufacturers have built craft which are variously suited as cruising or racing boats. Camper and Nicholsons are no exception and have provided the Three-Quarter Ton Cup boat—the **Nicholson 33**—in three versions. The hull design is by Ron Holland.

Built by Shipman Sweden AB, the **Norlin 34** is from the same designer's board as the very successful Scampi (see page 97). The 34 has been a race winner in the earlier marques over the Southern Ocean Racing Circuit. She is a recent winner of her class in the British Solent Points Championships and came second in her class in the Royal Ocean Racing Club Competition.

91

102: Norlin 37	L.O.A.	11·03m (36ft 2in)
	Beam	3·60m (11ft 10in)
	Draft	1·96m (6ft 5in)

Designed as a One Ton Cup contender, the **Norlin 37** is a maximum One Ton Cup design. She is a heavy displacement yacht with a large sail area. Being of fairly conventional design, she is as suitable for family cruising as for racing. Both the Norlin 34 and the 37 are similar in appearance, the 37 being a large version of the 34. Although the underwater profile is of little significance to the observer, the rudder is skeg-hung and the keel is an external lead keel with 4 per cent antimony to add hardness and strength.

In this range of craft there is also a **Norlin 41** which has a length overall of 12·46m (40ft 10in) a beam of 3·90m (12ft 10in) and a draft of 1·97m (6ft 6in). Powered with an auxiliary Volvo Penta 25 h.p. engine with a Hydromarin hydraulic drive and a shaft which emerges just aft of the keel, the vessel has an owner's cabin aft, equipped with a separate toilet compartment. The craft is not likely to be 'mass produced', being a rather exceptional and individual boat built very much 'to order'.

103: Norlin Accent

L.O.A.	8·00m	(26ft 3in)
Beam	2·75m	(9ft)
Draft	1·56m	(5ft 1in)

The **Accent,** also designed by Peter Norlin, was originally built without a coachroof (flush decked) for racing purposes. This version won the World Championship for the Quarter Ton Cup in 1974. As a result of the popularity of the craft and this win, a production version, with a raised coachroof, has been produced for cruising.

Designed by E.G. van de Stadt, the **Ocean 71** is the largest production glassfibre sailing vessel in the world. Apart from being a luxurious and spacious cruising craft she has proved her racing performance with such wins as the 2000 mile (two men only) Round Britain Race and the Cape Town to Rio Race. She is built by Southern Ocean Shipyard Ltd who also build smaller craft such as the Pioneer, a classic 9m (30ft) cruiser, which has been developed over the years since 1959.

104: Ocean 71

L.O.A.	21·64m	(71ft)
Beam	5·31m	(17ft 5in)
Draft	2·45m	(8ft 1in)

105: Ohlson 35 Mk II   106: Pandora International

L.O.A.	10·51m	(34ft 6in)	L.O.A.	6·65m	(21ft 10in)
Beam	3·20m	(10ft 6in)	Beam	2·10m	(6ft 11in)
Draft	1·83m	(6ft)	Draft	Varies according to keel	

Although a very competitive racing yacht in the Three-Quarter Ton Class, the **Ohlson 35** is also well equipped as a comfortable cruiser. Designed by Einar Ohlson, moulded by the Tyler Boat Co of England, she has, in recent years, won important races and championships. The **Mark II** version, benefiting from racing experience, was modified in the underwater body near the stern and in the rig height.

Pandora International and Prospect (not illustrated) are designed by E.G. van de Stadt. These craft have an unusual stowage for the outboard engine which is fitted in a neat well and can be hoisted out of the water. In this price range, and length of craft, there have to be compromises but there are many features of these two compact little cruisers to distinguish them. Although there is limited space below, it has been used to the best advantage.

107: Prelude			**108: Privateer**	

L.O.A.	5·86m (19ft 3in)		L.O.A.	5·98m (19ft 7½in)
Beam	2·09m (6ft 10in)		Beam	2·08m (6ft 10in)
Draft	dependent on keel		Draft	1·37m (4ft 6in)

Prelude, designed by Ian Proctor, being less than 6m (20ft) long, sports four full-length bunks and is typical, with her 'sister' ship the Pirate, of the small range of family cruiser. They can both be supplied with a fin keel or a drop keel, and in the case of Pirate with a third alternative, the twin bilge keel. Both craft can be easily trailed. Externally there is little to distinguish Pirate from Prelude which is illustrated.

From a design by Norman Howard, the styling of **Privateer** is on the lines of an American work boat in common use in Muscongus Bay about 1890. She is a centreboard craft, gaff or Bermudan rigged. With twin headsails, gaff main and topsail she provides easy and interesting sail work for a family crew including the children.

110: Sabre 27

L.O.A.	8·23m (27ft approx.)
Beam	2·8m (9ft)
Draft (fin)	1·4m (4ft 8in)
(twin bilge keel)	0·9m (3ft)

109: Rêve de Mer

L.O.A.	7·15m (23ft 3in)
Beam	2·5m (8ft 1¼in)
Draft (cruising)	1·10m (3ft 7in)
Draft (high performance)	1·40m (4ft 7in)

Rêve de Mer is designed by Group Finot, a French team of engineers and designers who achieved a high reputation with the successful Écume de Mer, the bigger sister of the Rêve. The vessel is constructed by Chantiers Mallard (of La Rochelle, France) with a tubular steel frame which gives a chassis effect athwartships to take the stresses and strains of the mast, its shrouds and the keel. As will be seen from the specification, the high performance version has a deeper keel. Both versions may be fitted with a Vire 7 h.p. 2-stroke engine. Rêve has an impressive list of wins in a variety of yacht races.

The **Marcon Sabre** has gained a number of awards in the family cruiser rallies and has some interesting internal design features. With a sail area, under mainsail and genoa, of 39m² (420ft²), she was designed by Alan F. Hill with an optional single fin keel or the twin bilge keels.

INTERNATIONAL CODE OF SIGNALS

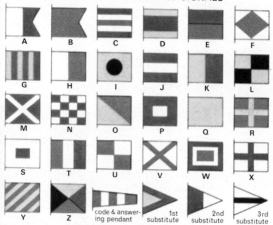

NUMERAL PENNANTS

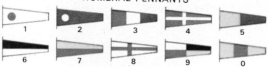

YACHTING FLAGS

A racing flag is rectangular, of any design, flown at the masthead (c)

A burgee is triangular; every yacht club has a different design

PLATE 1

International Code of Signals, Numeral Pennants and Yachting Flags: Special Yacht Club Flags (a) Flag of President, Past Commodore etc; (b) Commodore's Pennant; (c) Vice Commodore's Pennant; (d) Rear Commodore's Pennant

The Polish Training Ship *Pomorza* at Parade of Sail Cowes, Isle Wight, in 1974

U.S.C.G.C. *Eagle*. Built in 1936, she carries a crew of 65 and 110 cadets

PLATE 2

The Russian Barque *Kruzenshtern*. A four-masted Barque which has taken part in a number of 'Tall Ship' races

(*above*) *Unowot* leaps home to win the 1973 Cowes–Torquay International Offshore Powerboat Race. She also won in 1975 under the name *Unoembassy*, at an average speed of 72·86 m.p.h. over the 229 mile course

The Italian entry in the Cowes–Torquay – Cowes 1973 marathon on the final run past Portland Bill

PLATE 7

Blitz competing in the shorter Vectis Trophy Race, 1974

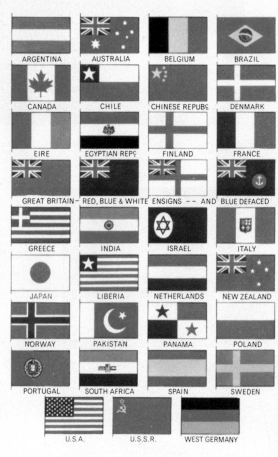

ARGENTINA	AUSTRALIA	BELGIUM	BRAZIL
CANADA	CHILE	CHINESE REPUBC	DENMARK
EIRE	EGYPTIAN REPC	FINLAND	FRANCE

GREAT BRITAIN — RED, BLUE & WHITE ENSIGNS — — AND BLUE DEFACED

GREECE	INDIA	ISRAEL	ITALY
JAPAN	LIBERIA	NETHERLANDS	NEW ZEALAND
NORWAY	PAKISTAN	PANAMA	POLAND
PORTUGAL	SOUTH AFRICA	SPAIN	SWEDEN
U.S.A.	U.S.S.R.	WEST GERMANY	

PLATE 8   National Flags and Ensigns

11: Scampi 30 Mk IV

L.O.A.	9·07m	(29ft 9in)
Beam	3·00m	(9ft 11in)
Draft	1·58m	(5ft 2in)

Peter Norlin designed the **Scampi 30** to compete in the Half Ton Class. In the 1971 Half Ton Cup the first three places fell to Scampi. Built by the Swedish firm Shipman Sweden AB, she was followed by the Quarter Tonner Lil' Scampi which also has achieved considerable success.

Peter Norlin has designed numerous other craft including the Norlin 34, 37 and 41.

Seal 22 is constantly being improved but the advantage of a lifting keel and rudder are manifest. The keel is raised by using a handle mounted on the rear of the trunking and is a well-engineered arrangement. The Seal 'Sinbad' is a de luxe version of the same vessel and has a 'well' for fitting an outboard engine of 6 h.p.

Angus Primrose designed this craft and also the Seal 27 which has seven berths. An 18 h.p. diesel engine is standard equipment.

112: Seal 22 Mk II

L.O.A.	6·63m	(21ft 9in)
Beam	2·36m	(7ft 9in)
Draft	1·21m	(4ft)

113: She S27 Mk III

L.O.A.   7·92m   (26ft)
Beam   2·59m   (8ft 6in)
Draft   1·45m   (4ft 9in)

Designed by Sparkman and Stephens and built by South Hants Marine, England, there are many examples of this craft which has proved a popular one in the smaller cruiser range. This is not to say that the **She S27** has not competed successfully in many races, however, and she continues to be, although relatively narrow beamed, a good performer and a good example of the classic design.

The **She S31b** was originally designed by Sparkman and Stephens as a fast 9m (30ft) cruising sloop but has latterly added many racing successes to her name. In the 1974 Cowes Week alone she notched up six firsts and two seconds.

The She 9·5 Traveller is a variant of the S31b with more headroom.

114: She S31b

L.O.A.   9·25m   (30ft   4½in)
Beam   2·70m   (8ft 10in)
Draft   1·65m   (5ft 5½in)

L.O.A. 10·72m (34ft)
Beam 4·57m (15ft)
Draft 0·84m (2ft 9in)

5: Snapdragon 27

O.A. 8·28m (27ft 2in)
eam 2·59m (8ft 6in)
aft 1·40m (2ft 9in)

116: Snowgoose Catamaran

The **Snapdragon 27,** from Thames Marine, Hamble, England, is a typical British cruiser for family use. She has a comparatively small mainsail in relation to her headsails. She carries 37m² (398ft²) of sail and has a convenient below-decks layout with a starboard side galley and dinette opposite. She is sold with either a fin keel or twin bilge keels.

Snowgoose Catamaran is cutter rigged. Between her twin hulls there is a canoe-shaped centre nacelle, which gives 2m (6ft 6in) headroom below. One of many 'multihull' cruisers, she offers a great deal of room. Her mast is set well aft; with small mainsail and large headsails she is easy to distinguish. Her mainsail is 15m² (161ft²) and, with two headsails, she has a total sail area of about 52m² (560ft²).

99

117: Sortilège

L.O.A.	12.50m	(41ft)
Beam	3·75m	(12ft 3in)
Draft	1·75m	(5ft 9in)

118: Swan 65

L.O.A.	19·7m	(64ft 8in)
Beam	4·9m	(16ft 4in)
Draft	2·8m	(9ft 3in)

One of the more famous names produced by the Michel Dufour S.A. company of La Rochelle, France, the **Sortilège** is illustrated in the optional ketch rigged version. She is an 8-berth cruiser and, in comparison with the Arpège from the same company, she carries 3·4 tons of ballast, being 3·25m (9ft 8in) greater in length overall. Fitted with an auxiliary engine of 43 h.p., she makes 7 knots under power and carries 80–90m² (861–969ft²) of sail.

Sayula II, a standard production **Swan 65,** became a household word in yachting circles when the vessel won the Whitbread Round the World Race. Rigged as a ketch, she has, for her size, a reputation for ease of sail handling. She can also be sloop rigged.

She was designed by Sparkman and Stephens and built by Nautor of Finland.

119: Swan 48		**120: Swan 44**	
L.O.A. sloop	14·64m (48ft)	L.O.A.	13·4m (44ft)
yawl	15·25m (50ft)	Beam	3·3m (12ft 6in)
Beam	4·15m (13ft 7¼in)	Draft	2·1m (7ft 2in)
Draft	2·36m (7ft 9in)		

The first of the class was completed in January 1972 and in that year **Swan 48** became a Bermuda race winner. The designers Sparkman and Stephens, and the builders Nautor of Finland have provided, in this craft, the alternative yawl rig. The hull is lengthened by 61cm (2ft) to accommodate the mizzen-mast aft.

The first **Swan 44** was completed in 1972. While winning races is as much to do with the crew and skipper as it is to do with the yacht's design, the Swan 44 gained the first four places in her class in the Bermuda Race, and one of the craft in the British winning team in the Southern Cross Series was a vessel of this marque. She also gained distinction as the R.O.R.C. Boat of the Year and Class I winner in 1974, as well as being selected as the 'Boat of the Show' at the London Boat Show and 'Boat of the Year' in Italy in 1973.

121: Swan 41		**122: Swan 38**	
L.O.A.	12·5m (41ft)	L.O.A.	11·58m (38ft)
Beam	3·64m (11ft 11in)	Beam	3·53m (11ft 7in)
Draft	1·98m (6ft 6in)	Draft	1·93m (6ft 4in)

The first **Swan 41** was completed in August 1973 and in the 1974 season she won various races. The 41 perpetuates the clean low-profile deck which is a feature of the larger vessels of this marque. Her engine is a Perkins Marine diesel fitted with an alternator to charge the starting and lighting battery supply.

Designed by Sparkman and Stephens and built by Nautor of Finland, the first **Swan 38** was completed in April 1974. It is an evolution from a long line of successful craft, amongst them the Swan 36 which competed in seven races at Cowes in 1968 and won all seven. Naturally specifications have changed during the years to suit, amongst other things, the I.O.R. rating rules.

123: Tornado 31

L.O.A.	9·20m (30ft 4in)
Beam	3·05m (10ft)
Draft	1·40m (4ft 7in)

124: Trapper 400

L.O.A.	8·6m (28ft 2½in)
Beam	2·54m (8ft 4in)
Draft	1·42m (4ft 8in)

From the American design team of Frank Butler and A. Garest Ltd, the **Tornado 31** (by the Spanish firm Playvisa) is a craft with a 3·05m (10ft) beam. This unusual width has many advantages and allows the accommodation to be spacious. She has sleeping berths for six or seven (depending on interior layout) with ample room for a big dinette area. The sail number 2343Y is a number issued by the Royal Yachting Association so that the yacht may be easily identified.

Designed by C & C Yachts, and built by Anstey Yachts, the **Trapper 400** has undergone a number of design changes including major alterations to the hull and deck, which entailed making new moulds. She carries, as a normal sail area, 29·10m² (312ft²) with the main (identical in area to the mainsail of the larger Trapper 500) being 12·17m² (129ft²).

125: Trapper 500

L.O.A.	8·33m	(27ft 4in)
Beam	2·8m	(9ft 2in)
Draft	1·45m	(4ft 9in)

126: Vega

L.O.A.	8·25m	(27ft 1in)
Beam	2·46m	(8ft)
Draft	1·17m	(3ft 10in)

Another craft designed by C & C Yachts and built by Anstey Yachts, **Trapper 500** has a displacement of 2·31 tons and a sail area under main and a large headsail of 29·45m² (approx: 312ft²). With a design which incorporates an unusually high coachroof, the boat is spacious and well strengthened.

Albin **Vega,** built by Albin Marin AB of Sweden and designed by Per Brohäll, at the time of going to press has achieved more than 2500 sales since its introduction in 1969. An International Class Association was formed and the yacht races in One-Design races. She is, for her size, a light displacement vessel of 2·3 tons. The stepped coachroof allows good head room to the fore cabin and the spray hood and high coamings provide a dry cockpit. Vega is fitted with a 10 h.p. 4-stroke 2-cylinder Volvo Penta MD 6A.

127: Vivacity 24   128: Warrior 35 Mk III

L.O.A.	6·34m (20ft 9in)	L.O.A.	10·67m (35ft)
Beam	2·44m (8ft)	Beam	3·20m (10ft 5in)
Draft (fin keel)	1·12m (3ft 8in)	Draft	1·52m (5ft)
(bilge keel)	0·76m (2ft 6in)		

Largest of the Vivacity range, the **24** gives good accommodation in a comparatively short hull and very adequate headroom below, without appearing to be too 'top heavy'. Designed by Alan Hill, she is touched by the American influence of big hatchways and windows which have many advantages when used as a family cruiser.

Designed by Angus Primrose, the **Warrior** can best be described as a successful motor-sailer. With a comparatively broad beam, she is extremely roomy and comfortable for her overall length, and with some models sporting a Mercedes 42 h.p. engine as standard, this is an excellent centre-cockpit craft, well capable of accommodating six people in comfort.

While the illustration depicts a sloop rig, she can be rigged as a yawl.

The Westerly range of cruisers built by Westerly Marine Construction Ltd of Waterlooville, Portsmouth, England, are well known throughout the world for the versatility of the various designs by Laurent Giles and Partners and for their sailing performance. Some of the designs, to the casual observer, are very similar (in some cases only the underwater shape is different).

The illustration is of the Westerly **Conway** which has, for example, three other variants. The **Conway** can be ketch or sloop rigged; the **Solway** is a shallow draft twin-keel version with an after-cabin, whereas the **Medway** is an aft-*cockpit*, sloop-rigged fin-keel version. The **Galway** is yet another variant. Externally their profile and construction are, of course, virtually indistingushable.

In any case, as the observer will discover, it is the

129: The Westerly Conway		
L.O.A.	10·89m	(35ft 9in)
Beam	3·41m	(11ft 2in)
Draft	1·83m	(6ft)

130: Centaur

L.O.A.	7·9m	(26ft)
Beam	2·6m	(8ft 5in)
Draft	0·9m	(3ft)

131: Pageant

L.O.A.	7·0m	(23ft 1in)
Beam	2·4m	(8ft)
Draft	0·85m	(2ft 10in)

very small details which distinguish craft by the same
designers when they are at sea. The sail insignia, of
course, is a ready means of identification. Compare,
for example, the **Pageant** and the **Centaur**. As the
manufacturers say, the **Pageant** is the smaller
version of the **Centaur**. Seen at sea, with the
Pageant a little closer than the **Centaur**, only very
minor details and a slightly different bow shape,
together with the sail insignia, will distinguish one
from the other.

The **Pageant** has a very large cockpit, relative
to its size. The **Centaur** is driven, when under
power, by the Volvo Penta MD2B 25 h.p. twin-
cylinder diesel. This is the engine used in the
majority of the Westerly range, and produces a
maximum speed, in this craft, of $6\frac{1}{2}$ knots, giving a
cruising range of 250 miles.

132: Longbow (sloop)

L.O.A.	9·5m	(31ft)
Beam	2·9m	(9ft 6in)
Draft	1·38m	(4ft 6in)

133: Berwick

L.O.A.	9·5m	(31ft)
Beam	2·9m	(9ft 6in)
Draft	1·1m	(3ft 7in)

The **Longbow** and the **Berwick** have similarities, the former being fin-keeled, the latter having twin bilge-keels and a skeg-hung rudder which makes her a good vessel for cruising in shallow waters.

The **Renown** (not illustrated) utilizes the **Longbow** hull, but the cockpit has been moved forward to provide a spacious after-cabin. Both can be supplied with sloop or ketch rig. The **Renown** is a fin-keel craft, whereas its 'sister ship', the **Pentland**, is a twin bilge-keeler, ketch rigged.

The drop-keel version of the **Westerly Jouster** (illustration **136**) provides a draft of 1·69m (5ft 7in) when lowered.

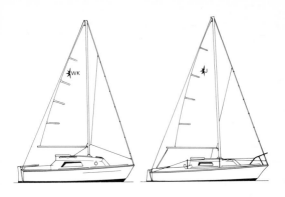

134: Warwick

L.O.A. 6·55m (21ft 6in)
Beam 2·35m (7ft 9in)
Draft 0·84m (2ft 9in)

135: Jouster

L.O.A. 6·4m (21ft)
Beam 2·28m (7ft 6in)
Draft 1·07m (3ft 6in)

Both the **Warwick** and the **Jouster** are in the small cruiser range and are suited to being trailed behind a car. While the 'drop-keel' version of the **Jouster** is hardly a handsome construction, it has many advantages and she has had racing successes. For the average family cruising man, the ability to take the boat home saves considerable expense.

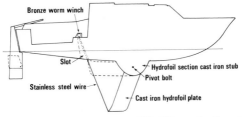

Bronze worm winch

Slot

Stainless steel wire

Hydrofoil section cast iron stub

Pivot bolt

Cast iron hydrofoil plate

136: Westerly Jouster

137: The Westerly Warwick loaded on a road trailer. This shows the configuration of the twin-bilge keel. The ability to 'take the ground' on the ebb-tide, clean the hull, and refloat on the flood saves money and time for the family cruising man.

138: The Tiger, designed by John Butler, is a handy 7·7m (25ft) family cruiser with racing potential. A fin-keeler in the lower price range, she is well balanced and carries 36m² (381ft²) of sail under main and genoa.

Chapter 9

SAILING DAYBOATS (DINGHIES AND KEELBOATS)

In a book of this length it is clearly not possible to illustrate every class of boat which has ever been constructed, but the selection of dayboats which follows is one based upon world-wide popularity, upon usefulness for training, for Olympic use, or for international competition. The internationally competitive craft which gain popularity in a number of countries are granted recognition by the International Yacht Racing Union and thereafter merit the word 'International' before their name.

Every country also has its special favourites which are not of International status. Many of the British National Classes have much in common with well-known national classes sailed in other countries. As the years go by, some of the finest designs diminish in popularity. Fashions change, and, with ever increasing prices, the fashion seems to be wending its way more and more to smaller boats which are capable of car-top transportation. Many well-tried designs have, however, stood the test of time. Originally of wood construction, they have been transformed and rejuvenated by the introduction of glass-reinforced polyester (G.R.P.) hulls, from a mould, which has helped manufacturers to keep prices at sane levels. The introduction of man-made materials for use as sail-cloth has also caused a revolution. Although it is still necessary to wash sails free of salt water and to dry them, they are relatively free from the risk of mildew, are lighter and easier to handle and to stow, and are certainly much stronger and less likely to 'blow out'.

In the pages which follow many of the well-known craft have started life as the result of sponsorship by

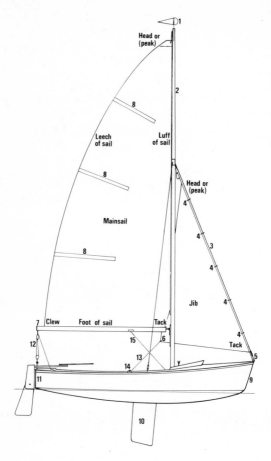

139: A side elevation of a dinghy (*see key opposite*)

newspapers, yachting magazines and, in some cases, by the National Authorities of the country of origin. The craft which have gained International status are first described, followed by those which, in many cases, have equal or greater international popularity, but which have not yet sought or been granted such status.

Every sport has its vocabulary. It is hardly surprising that sailing is full of unusual words seldom heard by the layman. The vocabulary of the sea is specific. A rope is never merely a rope but a sheet, a halyard, a kicking strap, a strop, a downhaul or uphaul etc. Each has a specific function and it is well that there should be no confusion! Many of the terms have been handed down from the days of commercial sail and, to this day, the sailors of different countries use orders which are recognizable in another language. Many of the names and orders used in modern-day yachting come from the mists of antiquity. **139** and **140** name the most essential parts of a dinghy, which is the most likely craft for the majority of people to use or see.

Key to illustration 139

1. Burgee (or if square— the racing flag)
2. Mast
3. Forestay
4. Jib hanks
5. Jib tack strop
6. Clew of jib
7. Boom
8. Battens in batten pockets. These are stiff pieces of wood or similar material inserted into batten pockets to stiffen the sail for greater efficiency
9. The bow. Also 'the stem' which was originally the piece of wood into which all the side planks were butted. Hence 'from stem to stern'
10. Centreboard, centre-plate (or dagger-board)
11. Stern
12. Mainsheet
13. Jibsheet
14. Jibsheet lead
15. Kicking strap

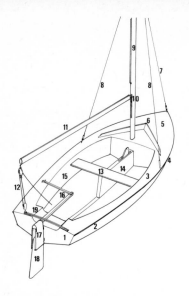

140 : The principal parts of a dinghy
1. Transom 2. Hull 3. Side deck 4. Rubbing strake 5. Foredeck
6. Washboard 7. Forestay (from bow to masthead) 8. Shrouds
9. Mast 10. Gooseneck 11. Boom 12. Mainsheet and blocks
13. Thwart 14. Centreboard case 15. Built-in buoyancy 16.
Tiller and tiller extension 17. Rudder stock 18. Rudder blade
19. After deck

The construction of a modern dinghy, of course,
varies from builder to builder, but **140** shows a typical
general type of construction. For simplicity many of
the details have been omitted in order to depict
adequately the bare essentials. Particularly note that
the foredeck, side-decks and after part of the craft
all form individual 'boxes' which are water-tight and
provide buoyancy if and when the craft capsizes. A
capsized dinghy will support its crew.

Development

The sport is one of constant innovation and many new ideas have been introduced in the last few years. These tend to make some racing craft over-sophisticated. Several of the individual Classes deliberately prohibit innovation in order to keep the craft, and racing, within the pocket of the average competitor. But in every sport there are participants who strive to achieve greater efficiency, faster speeds, higher heights or deeper depths. Sailing is no exception.

The interior of the cockpit of the Flying Dutchman depicted below indicates the lengths to which the sophisticated racing craft can be improved. Every piece of rope has a specific purpose. Apart from the obvious sheets for hauling in sails, and the equipment for 'trapezing', there are many 'tensioners' for various parts of the equipment. These may be for such purposes as adjusting the set of the sails for greatest efficiency on the different 'points' of sailing; adjusting the rake of the mast; slackening the foot of the sail; adjusting the tension of the rigging or to facilitate the setting of the spinnaker.

141: The interior of the cockpit of a **Flying Dutchman**, a class where the competition requires the ultimate in attention to detail and fine adjustment

142: The sophisticated arrangement for the setting of the spinnaker in a **Flying Dutchman**

In latter years spinnaker 'chutes' have become very much neater in design and the spinnaker can be set and lowered without the necessity for the crewman to leave the cockpit.

Centreboard, daggerboard or keel?

Every dinghy has a retractable keel which provides the necessary lateral resistance to the sideways movement induced by the pressure of the wind upon the sails. A centreboard is pivoted and can be raised by a system of ropes and pulleys as illustrated. A daggerboard, as its name implies, is merely raised and lowered by hand, as required. Keel boats have a fixed keel which cannot, of course, be adjusted.

143: *Left:* daggerboard. *Right:* centreboard or plate. Both are to provide lateral resistance to the thrust of the wind upon the sails

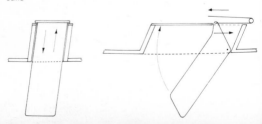

The adjustment of the movable keel in a dinghy is made according to the 'attitude' of sailing. If the craft is sailing close-hauled (as near to the direction of the wind as is possible) the centreboard will be fully down, because the lateral pressure is greatest and the maximum resistance is needed to stop the craft sliding sideways (making leeway). When sailing across the direction of the wind, the centreboard will be half lowered, and when running before the wind, there being hardly any sideways pressure, the board will be almost fully raised, to minimize unnecessary friction. So the observer will notice, if he is sufficiently close, that the helmsman and crew, apart from tending the sails and rudder, will also be adjusting the centreboard depth.

While the underwater shape of the hull is unlikely to be useful as an identification feature to the observer, there are very distinctive basic descriptions of the various methods of conventional hull construction.

A carvel-built boat is constructed with planking laid edge to edge on a framework and the finished product is smooth-sided. A clinker-built boat is one where the planking is overlapping. Both these types of construction will be seen.

Modern constructional methods also include the use of sheets of marine plywood, either cold-moulded or shaped in a steam press. The use of glass-reinforced polyester has revolutionized the construction of small boats which may be moulded in one piece to include buoyancy compartments, lockers, seats etc.

Round bilge

Single or hard chine

Double chine

144: The various shapes of dinghy hull

Controls

So that the boom may be controlled by the helmsman, it is necessary for the mainsheet to be led from the boat to the end or centre of the boom and back into the helmsman's hand. In small craft the pressure of wind in the mainsail is not very great and such craft will tend to have one block (or purchase) on the boom through which the mainsheet passes. Others will be sheeted 'there and back' two or three times. The pull which the helmsman exerts is then multiplied. This is very necessary with a large sail area. In some craft the pressure of wind-load may be great enough to require as many as three blocks (pulley wheels) on the boom. The illustration of a two-man catamaran clearly depicts this point of recognition. On many conventional craft an early point of recognition may be the number of 'purchases' visible as well, of course, as the shape of the hull and sails and the insignia on the sail (if this is immediately distinguishable).

145: The weight of wind in the mainsail of this catamaran requires a considerable number of purchases to enable the helmsman easily to control the mainsheet when sailing hard on the wind

Class racing

The majority of dayboats used in one-design class racing are built and carefully measured to very strict tolerances. There are minimum and maximum measurements for every part of the boat. On the other hand, there are also classes of boat where the rules of measurement are less strict and the owner may experiment within certain limits by redesigning, for example, the shape of the stern of his craft, or the method of sheeting his sails, or even adjusting the shape of his centreboard or rudder to minimize 'drag'. The three types are designated 'one-design', 'restricted', or 'development'. The whole intention of the class racing rules is to provide fair and equal competition within that class.

As a result of the latitude of design in certain classes it is sometimes hard to appreciate that the craft observed all belong to the same class, so radically different are they one from another. Equally, there are many classes where *no* variations are allowed and these will all have identical hulls and identical sail plans.

Sail numbers

There is a *certain* method of identifying craft while they are sailing which requires a word of explanation. Every class has its insignia which will be near the top of the sail. Each craft will have a number as well. If the owner sails in international competition there may also be a 'national' letter (for example, 'K' for United Kingdom, 'US' for United States of America). These are similar to the national plates worn on motor cars but are not the same.

In the pages which follow, the different sail insignia for each craft may be seen in the illustrations. A full list of the international letters is given in Appendix V.

In pursuit of speed

Particularly in the trimaran and catamaran types of hull, the ability to achieve high speeds is one of the main attractions, especially while racing! The conventional single-hull dinghy gives a great sensation of speed because of the proximity of the sea, but the average size of dinghy seldom achieves more than about 10 knots when sailing hard on the wind. With spinnaker, and wind and tide in favour, greater speeds can, of course, be achieved.

In the same way as the land-speed record could never be won by the conventional type of saloon motor car, the World Sailing Speed Record is likely to continue to be held by craft specially built for the purpose. The Flying Proa *Crossbow* was specially constructed with this aim and during 1975 established a new world record for sailing craft of over 31 knots. With her single hull, only about 0·5m (1ft 8in) across,

146: *Crossbow*, a **Flying Proa**, achieved more than 31 knots in 1975 during the World Sailing Speed Record Week

147: The Trimaran *Triple Arrow*, sponsored by a world-wide banking organization, met disaster and was found capsized 540 miles off the Canaries during a single-handed attempt to set up a 200-miles-a-day record

the crew occupy a 'sidecar' from which they can adjust the sails and steer the craft. As will be seen from a study of illustration **146**, the craft can only operate while sailing on the starboard tack. She is *very* specially built for the sole purpose of attacking sailing speed records.

A number of examples of the trimaran may be seen in the pleasure craft races of the world. A basic development from the days of the Polynesian outrigger, they are equipped with 'balancing' hulls constructed at the end of strong cross-members which, of course, take considerable strain when the vessel is being sailed hard. Notice in illustration **147** how the windward hull has already left the water. Notice also the small perpendicular vane at the after end of the centre hull which is the self-steering apparatus so continuously used, in one form or another, by lone sailors and for long passages when the crew must have time off from perpetually steering the boat.

Self-steering gear senses wind change, as does the weathercock on a church steeple. As it records a wind-shift it alters the rudder to compensate and keeps the vessel sailing. Without it an unattended yacht will tend to turn up into the direction of the wind and stop.

Over the years there have been many ingenious ideas to increase the speed of racing craft, not the least of which was a design of hull which could be lubricated to provide less friction of the wetted surfaces of the hull, following the 'design of nature' in such creatures as the dolphin! Rules as to the lubrication of hulls by mechanical or hand methods were soon introduced to avoid unfair competition.

The development of 'electronic gadgetry' has also received the attention of the rule makers. Imagine a racing yacht with a computer on board to work out best course and speed (to take account of tide and wind conditions) while the other craft in the race are still relying on the human brain and skill to win the race!

Dayboats which have been selected for inclusion in this section range from extreme designs to the humble 'built in the back garden' boat.

148: The **Trimaran FT** on trials in a Force 8 wind off Ramsgate on the East Coast of England

149: International Cadet		**150: International Canoe**	
L.O.A.	3·22m (10ft 6¾in)	L.O.A.	5·20m (17ft 0¾in)
Beam	1·27m (4ft 2in)	Beam	1·02m (3ft 4¼in)
Draft	0·76m (2ft 6in)	Draft	1·06m (3ft 6in)

Officially recognized as an International Class by the International Yacht Racing Union, this One Design class came into being immediately after World War II. She was specifically designed as a racing dinghy for crews aged between eight and seventeen years old. Admirably suited as a basic trainer for racing crews, the **Cadet** has been responsible for producing a number of top helmsmen. Designed by Jack Holt and promoted by *Yachting World* magazine, she remains a popular and relatively cheap racing craft, now built in G.R.P. She is known as a 'pram' dinghy because she has a square bow.

The International 10m² (approx. 108ft²) **Canoe** has been in existence for longer than any other 'dinghy'. Now subject to one-design restriction, the craft has a particularly identifiable configuration and is said to be one of the fastest of the single-handed mono-hull craft. The craft is now being built in G.R.P.

123

151: International Contender

L.O.A. 4·88m (16ft)
Beam   1·42m (4ft 8in)
Draft   1·37m (4ft 6in)

The **International Contender** is one of the craft more recently selected by the International Yacht Racing Union as an International Class. She is a high-performance single-handed racing craft which has attracted great interest, particularly in the United Kingdom, Australia and the United States. The three horizontal bars of her insignia are blue, red and blue. Apart from this recognition point there are five battens, the uppermost running right through to the mast. Since the helmsman spends most of his time supported out on the trapeze, he needs an unusually long tiller, which is another recognition point. Designed by Bob Miller, this craft has a large sail area and 'planes' easily, lifting most of her hull out of the water.

Compare now the **International Dragon** (**152**) which is one of the few *keel* boats included in the dayboat chapter of this book. She is world-renowned also and, despite the fact that she is no longer an Olympic Class, provides keen competition as a racing keel boat. She was designed, as a result of a competition, in 1929 by Johan Anker and built, in those days, for less than £100 sterling! She became an Olympic Class boat in 1948, the only alteration in her design being to the rigging plan which was changed in 1945.

The Dragon, a three-man keel boat of traditional Scandinavian design, was first introduced into Great Britain in the summer of 1935. In the following year the first series of International races took place and the Clyde Yacht Clubs presented the Dragon Gold Cup for competition, and continued to administer the class until 1946, when the administration was taken over by the British National Authority (R.Y.A.). There are large fleets in many countries with approximately 4000 craft registered.

The Dragon Class is a strict one-design class controlled by the International Yacht Racing Union and the boats must meet detailed specifications of material, measurement and weight. These regulations ensure the competitiveness of even the older boats. With a substantial list of builders, this good-looking, seaworthy aristocrat will continue to grace the scene for many decades to come.

152: International Dragon

L.O.A.	8·88m	(29ft 2in)
Beam	1·95m	(6ft 5in)
Draft	1·1m	(3ft 11in)

153: International Enterprise

L.O.A.	4·04m	(13ft 3in)
Beam	1·63m	(5ft 3in)
Draft	0·97m	(3ft 2in)

154: International Finn

L.O.A.	4·50m	(14ft 9in)
Beam	1·51m	(4ft 11¾in)
Draft	0·89m	(2ft 11in)

Perhaps one of the best known of the International Class boats, the **Enterprise** was designed by the very versatile Jack Holt. She is a double-chine Bermudan sloop, is enormously popular and extensively raced throughout the world. She is also a good training boat when sailed under cruising rig. She is almost instantly recognizable since the class rules require that the sails shall be dyed light blue.

The **Finn,** an International Class, made her début in the 1952 Olympic Games. The Una Bermudan rig, with unstayed rotating mast which can be 'flexed' to change the sail shape, and the tremendous competition among the young (and preferably heavy) helmsmen, have made this craft perhaps one of the most competitive racing machines. A single-hander, she provides the 'man-against-man' type of competition which makes a craft popular. She is a demanding craft and justifies her Olympic status.

155: International Fireball	**156: International Five–O–Five (5–0–5)**
L.O.A. 4·93m (16ft 2in)	L.O.A. 5·05m (16ft 6½in)
Beam 1·37m (4ft 6in)	Beam 1·90m (6ft 2½in)
Draft 1·22m (4ft)	Draft 1·14m (3ft 9in)

The **International Fireball** was designed by Peter Milne and has proved very successful since her introduction in 1962, especially since she can be built from a kit by prospective owners. She is almost a 'surfboard', and 'planes' extremely fast. Now professionally built with metal spars for those who wish to win, she provides excellent competition for two-men crews with 'trapeze' and spinnaker. Her insignia is a distinctive red ball.

The **5–0–5** is a craft which has achieved an enormous world-wide success as a high-performance two-man racing machine. Weighing a modest 127kg (280lb), she is light for her size and therefore demands a high degree of precise and expert helmsmanship. Developed in France, the rules of the class restrict the measurements of hull and rig, but quite substantial variations are permitted to suit individual preference.

157: International
Flying Dutchman

L.O.A. 6·05m (19ft 10½in)
Beam   1·70m (5ft 7in)
Draft   1·09m (3ft 7in)

158: International
Flying Junior

L.O.A. 4·04m (13ft 3in)
Beam   1·60m (5ft 3in)

The **International Flying Dutchman** was developed at the request of the International Yacht Racing Union and has the reputation of being the fastest two-man dinghy in the world. She is sailed competitively in most countries and is strictly one design, few variations being permitted for this boat which has been one of the Olympic Games Class of boats since 1960. She demands team-work between helmsman and crew (on a trapeze) because her sail area is large for her comparatively light construction. There are more than 4000 craft spread through thirty-five countries.

The **International Flying Junior** was designed by Uffa van Essen, the designer of the Flying Dutchman, as a training dinghy for the Flying Dutchman. She was awarded I.Y.R.U. International status as a good training craft for 'beginners'. Although she started life in Holland there are a number of fleets in the world, the largest being in the U.S.A.

159: International 470   160: International 14

L.O.A.	4·70m (15ft 5in)	L.O.A.	4·27m (14ft)
Beam	1·70m (5ft 7in)	Beam	1·42m (4ft 8in)
Draft	1·05m (3ft 5½in)	Draft	various

The **International 470** was designed by André Cornu of France and was originally exhibited at the Paris Boat Show in 1964. In Great Britain the class was slow to increase in numbers but there are now more than 15,000 of this strictly controlled one-design class for a crew of two. Once a boat has been selected to compete in the Olympics, the class can be assured of considerable expansion. She is now well known in France, the United States and Canada, to name but three countries. She is raced with spinnaker and trapeze and has proved herself an excellent seaboat.

The **International 14** was given International status as long ago as 1928. She is therefore the forerunner of many new ideas and could well be described as a 'test' machine belonging to a development class. The illustration is of one particular vessel, since hulls and rig may be of any shape or sort. They are used nowadays with trapezes and spinnakers.

161: International 420

L.O.A.	4·20m	(13ft 9in)
Beam	1·65m	(5ft 5in)
Draft	1·06m	(3ft 6in)

162: International Laser

L.O.A.	4·23m	(13ft 10½in)
Beam	1·37m	(4ft 6in)
Draft	0·76m	(2ft 6in)

The **International 420**, like the 470 and the 5–0–5, was named after her length overall (420cm). The designer, C. Maury, has produced a versatile training boat which was ultimately awarded International status. Her design allows of various rigs and she can therefore also be used for racing by experienced sailors. With spinnaker set, and the trapeze in use, she is a lively and likable racing craft.

The **International Laser** was designed by Bruce Kirby and has become, within the space of only four years, an International Class. Within three years from the commencement of production more than 20,000 were sold. The boat is a strictly one-design single-handed racing dinghy. To the casual observer, she is not unlike the International Finn, being Una Bermudan rigged. However she is smaller and her mainsail is loose-footed. Her total weight when sailing is only 68kg (150lb).

130

International Moth

	L.O.A.	3·34m (11ft)
	Beam (max)	2·25m (7ft 4in)
	Draft	Unrestricted

With a remarkable unrestricted 'restriction', as may be seen from the illustrations, this class has a development image. Hull shapes may vary from skiffs with 'wings' to tunnel hull scows. With a great number of sailing enthusiasts seeking improved performance, the class has always been popular and some 30,000 craft within the rules have seen the light of day. The sail insignia is the only infallible method of recognition.

163: An International Moth of the scow-hull design

164: An International Moth, designed as a skiff 'with wings', demonstrates the variation which the rules of this class allow

165: International O.K.　166: International Optimis

L.O.A.	4·00m	(13ft 2in)
Beam	1·42m	(4ft 8in)
Draft	0·82m	(2ft 8in)

L.O.A.	2·31m	(7ft 7in)
Beam	1·13m	(3ft 8½in)
Draft	0·71m	(2ft 4in)

Designed in 1954 as a 'trainer' for the International Finn, the **O.K.** gained International status in 1974. She is sailed in some 38 countries and is a one-design hard-chine Una Bermudan rigged dinghy. The mast has no support and rotates. The bend of the mast and sail-tension are altered by the helmsman according to requirement. Since there are more than 12,500 of these craft, it is one that is likely to be seen by the observer.

An International Class, flat-bottomed, hard-chine, pram-bow dinghy with a Una spritsail, this little vessel is world-renowned. A world-wide sail insignia has now been standardized but this craft is in any case quite unmistakable. With more than 42,000 examples in the world, **Optimist** is the beginner's boat, *par excellence*. Many fleets are raced by young crews, many of them competent sailors before the age of six! The illustration **166** is of the Veterans' Race, organized by children and sailed by their parents at a regatta at Karlskrona, Sweden.

167: International Soling   **168: International Snipe**

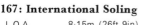

L.O.A.	8·15m (26ft 9in)		L.O.A.	4·72m (15ft 6in)
Beam (max)	1·90m (6ft 3in)		Beam	1·52m (5ft)
Draft	1·30m (4ft 3in)		Draft	0·99m (3ft 3in)

Designed in 1964 by Jan Linge, there are now more than 2500 of the **International Soling** Class, with more than 20 licensed builders throughout the world. An Olympic Class boat, she was entered in 1966 for the Three-man keel boat trials at Kiel, and adopted for the 1972 Olympics, where twenty-six countries entered. More than forty countries have affiliation to the International Association.

The **International Snipe** Class was designed in 1931 originally for amateur construction in plywood but can now be constructed in more modern materials. The hull shape is rigidly controlled by the rules, but variation in cockpit size etc, as well as choice of daggerboard or pivoting centreplate, is allowed. Over 22,000 are registered and the craft is raced in more than sixty countries, by all ages of helmsmen.

169: International Tornado

L.O.A.	6·10m	(20ft)
Beam	3·05m	(10ft)
Draft	0·76m	(2ft 6in)

170: International Tempest

L.O.A.	6·69m	(21ft 11¾in)
Beam	1·97m	(6ft 5½in)
Draft	1·10m	(3ft 7in)

One of the most successful of the catamaran type of craft, the **Tornado** was granted International status very quickly after its conception in 1966. In 1972 it was accepted as one of the Olympic classes. More than a quarter of the total of over 2000 in the class are German registered, but other countries, such as the U.S.A., United Kingdom, Canada and Australia, have large fleets. The vessel is sailed in twenty-nine countries and has attracted many expert sailors from other classes.

The **Tempest** was designed by Ian Proctor to fulfil a need for a modern international, high-performance, two-man planing keel boat. The first mould was produced in 1966 and she was chosen as an Olympic Class boat for the 1972 Olympics, where she was sailed by twenty-one nations. She competed again in the 1976 Olympics. Especially in the years 1965–1969, she won many One-of-a-kind races in France, U.S.A., and the United Kingdom.

171: International Vaurien

L.O.A.   4·08m (13ft 4½in)
Beam   1·45m (4ft 9in)
Draft   0·96m (3ft 2in)

Vaurien was designed by Jacques Herbulot in 1951 as a boat suitable for beginners and also for racing. She became extremely popular in her home country France, and more than 30,000 sail numbers exist in Europe. Like many other craft she was first constructed in plywood but more recent versions are in G.R.P. She is extensively used for training purposes. She has a hard-chine (flat-bottomed) hull and a dagger-board.

The **International Star** and the **International Echelles 22** are little seen in British waters but have gained a certain popularity in other countries.

172: The International Star

173: The International Echelles 22

174: Albacore

L.O.A.	4·58m	(15ft)
Beam	1·60m	(5ft 3in)
Draft	1·45m	(4ft 9in)

175: Bonito

L.O.A.	4·42m	(14ft 6in)
Beam	1·22m	(4ft)
Draft	0·71m	(2ft 4in)

The world-renowned Uffa Fox originally designed a sailing boat called a Swordfish, and from that hull design was developed the **Albacore.** This very successful British National Class boat was originally built by Fairey Marine, using plywood in the 'hot moulded' method of construction which involves steaming and pressing the material into the moulded shape of the hull. Albacore made her appearance about 1954 and was granted National status in the United Kingdom in 1963. She is one-design and is seen in large numbers in the United Kingdom, U.S.A. and Canada.

A single-handed racing craft, **Bonito** is ideal for holidays and casual sailing. She has a considerable stem with a deep 'V' conformation and is designed with an open transom. The unbattened sail is sleeved over an unstayed, sectionalized alloy mast and she is therefore admirably suited to 'car-top' travel. A variety of sail colours will be seen, the more modern having white sails. Earlier craft, as seen in the illustration, have red-and-white striped sails.

176: Bosun

L.O.A.	4·27m (14ft)
Beam	1·68m (5ft 6in)
Draft	0·99m (3ft 3in)

177: Cherub

L.O.A.	3·66m (12ft)
Beam (max)	1·54m (5ft)
Draft (max)	1·83m (6ft)

Designed by Ian Proctor, the **Bosun** is a typically well-designed 'training' dinghy. She has rounded side decks and was designed specifically for use by the British Royal Navy for training purposes. She is suitable for a crew of up to four, being equipped with virtually maximum buoyancy for a craft of this size. Now extensively used by many educational and training establishments with a working rig, she is capable of carrying a larger headsail to increase performance and is raced as well as being used for training.

The design of the **Cherub** is interestingly unrestricted. Any material may be used, the original concept being in plywood. With no restriction on the beam measurement at the stern, many variations of hull shape are possible. Sails may be battened in various ways and she is sailed with trapeze and spinnaker. The craft was first sailed in New Zealand but her use has spread to other countries, notably the United Kingdom and United States.

137

178: C-Lark

L.O.A. 4·27m (14ft)
Beam 1·70m (5ft 8½in)
Draft 1·06m (3ft 6in)

179: Drascombe Dabber

L.O.A. 4·72m (15ft 6in)
Beam 1·79m (5ft 10in)
Draft 0·91m (3ft)

The **C-Lark** was designed in 1964 by Don Clark and is an easy-handling day sailer which has reached considerable numbers on the North American continent. Most of the craft are to be found in the United States of America but there are a few in British Columbia. She is designed for quick self-righting and is by no means an out-and-out racer. She is, however, an exceptional training boat and is widely used for that purpose in junior and college sailing programmes. She is a tough little boat, well designed for beaching or trailer use.

Reminiscent of the clinker-built beach boats used by fishermen, the **Dabber** can be sailed without a mainsail in heavy weather. She can be equipped with a lugsail or spritsail and is the smallest of the sailing boats in this well-known range designed by J.L. Watkinson for the family sailing boat. The reefing points on the main can be lowered slightly and the sail area diminished as required.

181: Drascombe Lugger

L.O.A. 5·64m (18ft 6in)
Beam 1·91m (6ft 3in)
Draft 1·22m (4ft)

180: Drascombe Driver

L.O.A. 5·50m (18ft)
Beam 1·88m (6ft 1½in)
Draft 0·43m (1ft 5in)

The **Driver** is a motor-sailer with a long central keel, deepening at the after end to protect the propeller. The vessel is bilge-keeled and yawl-rigged. The mainsail is a loose-footed standing lugsail. The illustration is of a Driver in Biscayne Bay, Florida.

The **Drascombe Lugger** dayboat was designed with a yawl rig by J.L. Watkinson and has been extensively used as a training boat and as a cruising boat. With an uncluttered cockpit and plenty of stowage space and buoyancy, she is perhaps the best known of this extensive range of craft, and has been used not only as a training boat, for which she is well suited, but for extended cruising.

182: Eighteen

L.O.A. 5·49m (18ft)
Beam 1·83m (6ft)
Draft 1·37m (4ft 6in)

183: Firefly

L.O.A. 3·66m (12ft)
Beam 1·42m (4ft 8in)
Draft 1·07m (3ft 6in)

This British National Class boat was first designed by Uffa Fox, commissioned by the magazine *Yachting World*. In 1938 the **18** was adopted by the then British Yacht Racing Association and is still a National Class. Other designs by Bob Anderson, Jack Holt and Ian Proctor have since appeared. The purpose of the class is to provide a fast racing boat to be sailed by a crew of up to three in number. The boat is half-decked and can be built in modern materials.

The sail insignia is the number **18,** which provides immediate recognition.

The **Firefly** has been a very successful dinghy with British National status since her introduction in 1946. She comes from the drawingboard of Uffa Fox and was originally constructed in large numbers by Fairey Marine, using the hot moulded method of construction in plywood. After many changes of rules she can now be built in G.R.P. She is a strictly one-design class and has served as a 'nursery' for many well-known sailors.

140

184: Flying Fifteen

L.O.A. 6·10m (20ft)
Beam 1·54m (5ft)
Draft 0·76m (2ft 6in)

185: G.P. 14

L.O.A. 4·27m (14ft)
Beam 1·53m (5ft)
Draft 0·91m (3ft)

The **Flying Fifteen** is a British National Class boat designed for two-man sailing by Uffa Fox. When out of the water, her distinctive 'bulb' keel helps recognition. She is raced extensively throughout Great Britain. She is a One-Design Class and can be built only within strict parameters (of either wood or G.R.P.). Apart from her extensive use at over fifty centres in the British Isles, she is sailed in some thirty other countries.

G.P. 14 was designed by Jack Holt. With a hard-chine hull she was originally designed for construction in wood but the class adopted G.R.P. construction in 1967. Commissioned by the magazine *Yachting World*, she has national associations in many countries and there are around 10,500 of these craft in the United Kingdom. The bell insignia is also seen in Australia, the United States and South Africa.

186: Graduate	**187: Gull Mk III**
L.O.A. 3·81m (12ft 6in) Beam 1·42m (4ft 8in) Draft 1·17m (3ft 10in)	L.O.A. 3·34m (11ft) Beam 1·60m (5ft 3in) Draft 0·91m (3ft)

Originally sponsored by the magazine *Light Craft*, the **Graduate** gained National status in Great Britain in 1967, some fifteen years after she first appeared. She is typical of the popular dinghy used in schools and training establishments. The administration of the class is organized on a regional basis. With some 2500 in existence and sundry championships for schools, juniors and adults, and construction in G.R.P. this is a continuing class.

Originally designed by Ian Proctor as a double-chine dinghy for youngsters, the very successful **Gull** is now built in G.R.P. with a round-bilged hull. Despite the changing design-details of the various marques since the introduction of this craft, she is eminently suitable for teaching beginners, especially children.

142

188: Heron

L.O.A. 3·42m (11ft 3in)
Beam 1·37m (4ft 6in)
Draft 0·91m (3ft)

189: Hornet

L.O.A. 4·88m (16ft)
Beam 1·40m (4ft 7in)
Draft 1·32m (4ft 4in)

Jack Holt was commissioned by *Yachting World* in
1951 and **Heron** is the result. Originally designed for
amateur construction from kits, inevitably the later
versions are G.R.P. and professionally built. Unusually, her rig is gunter sloop, rather along the lines of
the later Mirror dinghy, also designed by Jack Holt.
The craft has National status in Australia and she is
well in evidence in many other countries.

A British National Class, **Hornet** was designed by the
ubiquitous Jack Holt, again commissioned by *Yachting World* magazine. Now being sailed with trapezes,
large genoas and spinnakers, she is very fast and very
popular in many countries. Many craft will be seen
with a sliding seat instead of the trapeze. She is distinctive with a tall, relatively narrow, mainsail (high
aspect ratio). The sail has four battens and the vessel
has a nearly perpendicular bow.

190: Javelin

L.O.A. 5·36m (17ft 7in)
Beam 1·68m (5ft 6in)
Draft 1·30m (4ft 3in)

191: Kestrel

L.O.A. 4·75m (15ft 7in)
Beam 1·68m (5ft 6in)
Draft 1·26m (4ft 1½in)

Javelin was designed by the well-known British designer Peter Milne and is distinctive because of her length, high aspect ratio mainsail and centrally located mainsheet. Although she is mainly seen round the south and east coasts of Great Britain, examples of the craft are also sailing in Germany, Holland and Austria. Sailed with a trapeze, she is extremely manoeuvrable and gives a good planing performance for her two-man crew.

Designed (specifically for G.R.P. construction) by Ian Proctor, **Kestrel** is round-bottomed for ease of construction. The design was produced in the 1950s but the first craft out of the mould did not appear until 1960. Since then, the class has been growing quite rapidly and examples of this two- or three-man dinghy will be seen in a number of countries where fleets are becoming established.

192: Lark

L.O.A. 4·06m (13ft 6in)
Beam 1·68m (5ft 6in)
Draft 1·14m (3ft 9in)

193: Leader

L.O.A. 4·27m (14ft)
Beam 1·65m (5ft 5in)
Draft 1·07m (3ft 6in)

A round-bilged one-design dinghy. **Lark,** designed by Mike Jackson, provides an interesting comparison with many other craft. With a comparatively light hull, she carries a relatively small sail area and therefore provides a good 'training' potential for novice crews. She was deliberately designed with the idea of a competent helmsman and inexperienced crewman in mind.

Leader is easily recognizable by the blue panel at the head of her sail. She was designed by D. Mace and J. Pollard for use as a family dinghy with racing potential, and is admirably suited for use as a training boat. She is sensibly priced and has a potential for considerable expansion. A beamy craft, she is a good choice as a family boat.

194: Merlin Rocket	**195: Minisail**
L.O.A. 4·27m (14ft)	L.O.A. 3·96m (13ft)
Beam 2·11m (6ft 11in)	Beam 1·12m (3ft 8in)
Draft various	Draft 0·76m (2ft 6in)

This British National Restricted Class evolved from the Jack Holt designed Merlin which was 'launched' in 1946, later to be amalgamated with the Rocket. The **Merlin Rocket** Class was granted national status in 1951 and has been one of the continually developing classes ever since. The racing competition within this class has always been keen and the class has produced a number of internationally known yachtsmen. Within the rules there are many variations possible. Note in illustration **194** of No. 2607 the pronounced shape of the sail at the top batten.

Minisail is a sailing surfboard with a shallow hull and a scow bow. One of an increasing number of Una Bermudan craft with a sail sleeved on to an unstayed mainsail, she can be fitted with a sliding seat and provides exhilarating racing potential. One of the fastest growing racing classes in the United Kingdom, she is ideal for 'car-topping'. The recognition of a white sail with red or orange stripes is easy.

146

196: Miracle

L.O.A. 3·88m (12ft 9in)
Beam 1·52m (5ft)
Draft 1·06m (3ft 6in)

197: Mirror

L.O.A. 3·30m (10ft 10in)
Beam 1·41m (4ft 7½in)
Draft 0·76m (2ft 6in)

Coming between the Mirror dinghy and the Mirror 14 in size, the **Miracle** was designed last and has a novel method of home construction, rather more simple than the original Mirror's 'wire stitch and glue' method. The transverse members have lugs which are fitted into slots on the longitudinal members. Once the glue and resin have set, the lugs may be sawn off. Still in its infancy at the time of going to press, this Jack Holt design is a worthy companion to the highly successful Mirror.

This hard-chine dinghy with a pram bow has achieved international success following its sponsorship by the *Daily Mirror* newspaper. Designed by Jack Holt and Barry Bucknell, **Mirror** appeared in 1963 as a do-it-yourself construction kit with plywood panels 'stitched' with wire and seamed with glassfibre tape and resin. She is a gunter sloop with distinctive red sails. Sail numbers are, at the time of going to press, somewhere near the 50,000 mark.

198: Osprey

L.O.A. 5·33m (17ft 6in)
Beam 1·77m (5ft 9in)
Draft 1·47m (4ft 10in)

199: Pacer

L.O.A. 3·8m (12ft 7in)
Beam 1·4m (4ft 8in)
Draft 1·12m (3ft 8in)

The **Osprey** has an unusual hull shape—treble chine —and has a relatively tall mast for her length. Early models used to have the mast strengthened by 'spreaders' in order to support extra rigging. The long after-deck is a very distinctive feature of this British National Class dinghy, designed by Ian Proctor as a high-performance two-man dinghy.

The **Pacer,** first named Puffin Pacer, designed by Jack Holt, is a successful double-chine hull craft, for amateur construction in wood, or professionally built in G.R.P. Points of recognition are the insignia (the International Code Flag 'P'), a long top batten which pushes the mainsail leech out at an angle and the dark blue sails. Earlier craft may have a Puffin as insignia.

200: Scorpion

L.O.A. 4·27m (14ft)
Beam 1·47m (4ft 10in)
Draft 1·04m (3ft 6in)

201: Shearwater III

L.O.A. 5·03m (16ft 6in)
Beam 2·28m (7ft 5in)
Draft 0·18m (7in)

T.J. Darling designed the **Scorpion** which was granted National status in the U.K. in 1967 as the 14ft One-Design Class. She is built in either G.R.P. or wood and, equipped with spinnaker and being fairly light, can 'plane' easily. With quite radical differences in cockpit design allowed by the rules, she has proved a popular boat, particularly on inland waters, reservoirs and gravel pits.

Shearwater has National status in the United Kingdom and has developed since 1957. With its twin catamaran hulls it is claimed to reach up to 20 knots in strongish winds. The Mark III is a G.R.P. version of the original design by Francis and Roland Prout. There should be little difficulty in recognition. With six battens (as shown in the illustration) and the twin hulls the craft should be unmistakable.

149

202: SigneT

L.O.A.	3·78m (12ft 5in)
Beam	1·45m (4ft 9in)
Draft	1·02m (3ft 4in)

203: Solo

L.O.A.	3·77m (12ft 4½in)
Beam	1·52m (5ft)
Draft	0·91m (3ft)

Ian Proctor designed the **SigneT** dinghy for one-design racing and there are now fleets in the U.K., Western and South Australia, Victoria, British Columbia and the U.S.A. In 1961 the *Sunday Times* sponsored this craft but, once established, she soon became popular for building by amateurs, and by schools and other groups. She is light and easily carried on car-top or behind a light car. As a cruising boat, she can be fitted with a small outboard motor.

The **Solo** has British National Class status. She is Una-Bermudan rigged with a double-chine hull. Designed by Jack Holt, she is used for racing in fleets throughout the United Kingdom and is well represented in Holland and Canada. She is a lively little single-handed craft. Strictly one design, she may be distinguished by the full-length battens running right from the after edge (the leech) of the sail to the mast.

204: Squib

L.O.A. 5·79m (19ft)
Beam 1·87m (6ft 2in)
Draft 0·91m (3ft 3in)

205: Sunfish

L.O.A. 4·22m (13ft 10in)
Beam 1·22m (4ft)
Draft Surfboard

Designed in 1968 and a National Class boat in the United Kingdom, **Squib** is a keelboat with a displacement of 682kg (1503lb) and is sailed in the major centres in Great Britain. The stability of a keelboat has many advantages for the family day-sailer but the craft is raced keenly and competitively with spinnaker. She has an iron keel weighing 341kg (752lb). The brown sails and the long fore-deck assist recognition, as does the relatively small cockpit and the slightly raised 'cuddy' on the fore-deck.

The **Sunfish** has a daggerboard but she is less extreme than her companion 'ship' the Sailfish which is the most popular of the sailing surfboards and satisfies a huge demand in the United States of America. The Sunfish has a hard-chine G.R.P. hull with a 'V' bottom and the rig is lateen. The illustration was taken during the first Sunfish World Championship when fifty-six contestants took part from eleven countries.

151

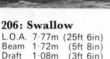

206: Swallow
L.O.A. 7·77m (25ft 6in)
Beam 1·72m (5ft 8in)
Draft 1·08m (3ft 6in)

207: Swordfish
L.O.A. 4·57m (15ft)
Beam 1·52m (5ft)
Draft 1·45m (4ft 9in)

The **Swallow** keelboat, designed by Tom Thornycroft in 1946, was selected as the Two-man Keelboat for the 1948 Olympics, and was the craft in which a Gold Medal was won for Great Britain. Built now in G.R.P., she has lost none of her beauty and can be seen gracing the waters of the Solent off Cowes and in the adjacent estuarial waters. Unusually for a keelboat, she is quite capable of reaching sufficient speed to 'plane' when sailing off the wind.

The **Swordfish** may catch the observer out with her sail insignia of **15** but that refers to her length and she is the British National Class at that length. She is unlikely to be seen in any great quantity since the class has been very severely restricted as a result of the development of the Albacore from the same manufacturer, Fairey Marine. The Albacore is basically a Swordfish hull with a greater sail area, and the two craft are indeed very similar.

208: (National) 12

Maximum length   3·66m (12ft)
Minimum hull weight 90kg (200lb)

209: Wayfarer

L.O.A. 4·83m (15ft 10in)
Beam 1·85m (6ft 1in)
Draft 1·17m (3ft 10in)

Granted National status in the United Kingdom, the **National 12** Class (sail insignia '**N**') is a development class and has been for the last 40 years! Construction can be in wood (clinker or butted) or in G.R.P. As the rules are not rigid, design of hull can be almost any shape or size within certain basic definitions. Designers, some amateur, are always experimenting. The class was originally formed as a 'feeder' for the International 14.

Designed by Ian Proctor, the **Wayfarer** is perhaps most widely used for instructional purposes. She is roomy, tough and seaworthy, and has been used for some remarkable cruising voyages. She is also a good family boat. With a Bermudan sloop rig she can carry a spinnaker and is therefore used for racing. National Associations of this class abound and she is known from Scandinavia to the United States.

153

210: 'X' One Design (XOD)

L.O.A. 6·33m (20ft 9½in)
Beam 1·82m (6ft)
Draft 0·84m (2ft 9in)

Certainly in Great Britain there is a breed of One-Design boats which deserve inclusion in this book for no other reason than longevity. Many 'local' One Designs, like the 'X' boat, perpetuate the delight in the craftsman's skills and in being unashamedly and proudly made of wood.

The 'X' boat was designed in 1909 by Alfred Westmacott, a Naval Architect, and the first was built in the finest woods for less than £50 sterling. A clinker-built iron-keeled boat which still graces Cowes Week as a competitive racing craft although it was designed more than sixty-five years ago, the XOD is now of historical importance.

Originally fitted with a gaff rig, in 1928 the class rules were altered to allow Bermudan rig, upon which a number of owners resigned from the class! Standing rigging originally included two backstays with runners but in company with many other older boats, the class has now shortened the boom, and allowed a more modern standing backstay. These changes are bound to come but the original design remains virtually intact. Prior to 1939 yachts were planked with pitch pine but later craft are built of mahogany planking, except those built locally in Kuwait where the planking is of teak!

154

Chapter 10

POWERBOATS

In the following pages only a cross-section of the many hundreds of available makes of powerboats are depicted. They have been selected for their different characteristics. Powered pleasure craft, many of which are used in commercial, as well as pleasure, roles are perhaps more numerous throughout the world than sailing boats. The various types have their individual purpose and, probably more important, their individual limitations. The craft which may have been selected with the sheltered harbour area in mind may be less than ideal for difficult tidal waters.

Hull Shapes

Powered craft can be divided into two main types: the displacement craft and the planing craft. The displacement craft's hull remains immersed and, whatever the power of the engine, there is a maximum speed beyond which it will not go. The immersed hull merely creates a larger and larger wave as it reaches its maximum speed. The hull form is basically rounded, rising upwards and inwards at the stern. The planing craft's hull is shaped quite differently. The lines are straighter, and tend to flatten the stern wave, with the result that the bows of the craft lift out of the water. This type of craft, with a good deal

211 : The Fairey Marine Fantôme is powered by twin diesels giving a top speed, in the cruising version, of some 30 knots, and is typical of the deep 'V' planing-hull con-figuration.

of its hull out of the water, will go faster than a displacement craft with the same power of engine. However, there is also a maximum speed for planing craft, and it is useless to use a larger engine than will suit the design.

Inflatable craft (with outboard engines) are also planing craft and are hard to beat for simplicity, low cost and safety. Later developments, using a glass-reinforced plastic deep 'V' hull bonded to multi-compartment inflated topsides, produce very similar handling characteristics to the larger offshore power-boat.

At the high-speed end of the range of planing craft are the racing hydroplanes, suitable only for sheltered waters, capable of reaching speeds of more than 100 m.p.h. These, for their size, have relatively enormous engines.

The craft used for the top competition in the International Cowes–Torquay Offshore Powerboat Race are custom built for racing and require anything up to 1200 h.p. to drive them at speeds around the 60 knot range. Such craft provide experience in the design of safe and seaworthy, fast family cruisers.

212: The Glastron GT 160, a typical 16ft sportsboat

213: *Miss Embassy*, turbine-driven Off shore Powerboat co tender, pictured here the 1973 Cowes–To quay Offshore Powe boat Race

Engines

When a boat is large enough, whether displacement or planing, the inboard diesel engine provides the greatest reliability coupled with minimum fire risk. The modern diesel (with an exhaust-driven turbo compressor which supplies extra air for combustion) is, perhaps, the most dependable and economical.

For convenience, the trailer-drawn boats and small cruisers are usually powered by outboard engines, which are complete units in themselves, capable of being easily removed from the craft for stowage or servicing. The majority of the larger ones have separate fuel tanks stowed inside the boat and connected to the engine by flexible fuel pipes. These are nearly all 2-stroke engines requiring a petrol/oil mixture.

Many boats are fitted with what are described as 'outdrive units'. These retain the two advantages of the inboard and the outboard engine. In effect, these engines are the lower half (propeller end) of an outboard, connected through the transom of the craft to a fully installed inboard engine usually driven by petrol. The more sophisticated versions are lifted by hydraulic power so that as the craft nears, for example, a beach the driver can raise the propeller out of the water to avoid grounding.

Clearly, vessels with this capability cannot also have a rudder, and the steerage of this sort of craft and of all outboard craft is maintained by altering the angle of thrust of the engines; whereas, in the conventional propeller-driven boat, the propeller is usually mounted forward of the rudder to give maximum water-flow past the rudder and therefore maximum steerage.

For certain applications the water-jet engine has many advantages, although all steerage is lost when the power in this type of unit is shut down. The engine, either petrol or diesel, is situated in the normal place inboard and drives either an axial or mixed-flow pump. The entire output of the engine is used to draw in water, accelerate it and to discharge it at high speed through a stern jet-pipe somewhat similar to the use of airflow in a jet aircraft. As the water leaves the jet-pipe it can be deflected *sideways* to alter the direction of travel and, in the latest, most sophisticated units, *vertically* in order to alter the fore and aft trim of the vessel. The obvious application of such engines, there being no moving parts on the exterior of the hull, is in shallow waters, where rocks, coral heads, weed and other hazards are present.

Design for specific use

In many cases the designers of pleasure boats have found a commercial application for those originally designed purely for pleasure. Many of the craft described in this book have been sold for multifarious uses, even finding a role as high-speed assault craft in a military application.

It is clearly not possible in a book of this length to discuss all the different 'makes' available from the markets of the world. However, a selection has been made which demonstrates the enormous variety of craft available. Perhaps one of the most important aspects of pleasure boating is that the correct type of craft must be chosen for the specific use. Many craft are specifically designed for river or very close inshore use in estuaries and the like. Only the foolhardy would use these in a deep-sea environment. Vessels with only one engine are not appropriate for use on long sea voyages for obvious reasons of mechanical failure. Hence, if the reader is perspicacious, 'design for use' will also form a part of his interest in the craft described in the following pages.

Avon Inflatables

One of the leading manufacturers of inflatable boats, this company produces a range of fully inflatable **yacht tenders** made from heavy duty nylon/hypalon. The material is treated to resist petrol, abrasion and sunlight. The technique of construction is to provide an inflatable tubular hull. Virtually unsinkable, even when swamped, the craft are stable, seaworthy and very portable. In the **sportsboat** range, the tubular construction forms the bow and sides and there is a flat rigid sternboard upon which to mount the engine.

Avon Seariders are constructed with a deep 'V' glassfibre hull, bonded to the buoyancy tubes. The SR4M (**214**) can carry an engine of maximum 50 h.p. and, apart from sport use, serves many operational uses such as H.M. Coastguard work.

Beaufort Inflatables

Beaufort (Air-Sea) Equipment Ltd (**215**) provide a range of craft from 2·43m (8ft) to 3·96m (13ft). As tenders, sportsboats or as rescue equipment, some can be fitted with inflatable keels, which add to stability. Fibreglass or marine ply floors create rigidity and can be fitted to most of the craft.

The sports boats 330 GT and 400 GT are designed to carry a steering wheel and cable controls. Maximum speeds are 32 to 34 m.p.h. respectively.

214: The Avon Searider—SR4M

215: Part of the Beaufort range

216: The Bertram 35 Convertible

217: The Bertram 38

Bertram

The Bertram range is a highly versatile and well constructed selection of deep 'V' hull craft. The company pursue a policy of offering alternative superstructures to each hull size. The 26ft Sport Convertible has a cockpit length of 2·7m (8ft 9in) and forward accommodation. The 26ft Hardtop is similar but has a coachroof extending well aft. The pleasant 28ft Flybridge Cruiser is powered either by twin 233 h.p. Mercruisers or 225 h.p. Chrysler engines.

The 35 (**216**) is called the Convertible. With a beam of 4·00m (13ft) she is stable and deep-sea proven. She is powered by twin 350 Mercruisers, or Cummins 240 h.p. diesels. A third variation of power unit is with twin 225 h.p. Caterpillar diesels. The company also provide a 38ft craft of similar configuration (**217**).

The Bertram 42ft (**218**) has a completely different configuration with the bridge set well aft. She is powered by 320 h.p. Cummins diesels or 335 h.p. 6–71TI Incline G.M. diesels.

218: The Bertram 42

219: Boston Whaler Outrage 21

L.O.A. 6·5m (21ft 4in)
Beam 2·23m (7ft 4in)
Draft 0·64m (2ft 1½in)

Boston Whalers

Boston Whalers Inc of Massachusetts make a range of craft from 11ft to the Outrage 21ft which is illustrated. All are virtually unsinkable and of great hull strength. Their uses range from rescue to fishing. The mainly flat hull is specially shaped at the bow end so that when the craft is at rest or in a following sea she is very stable. The majority of the range are powered by one outboard and have rails round the bow to avoid children or dogs falling over, with obviously fatal results!

Boston Whaler Outrage 21 was designed for a maximum of 200 h.p. Various power units may be fitted. For safety two 50 h.p. engines would be recommended, both with separate fuel tanks and supply lines.

Broom Cruising craft

The **Broom 35** is the middle of a range of craft built by this British company. The smallest (not illustrated) is the 30 which is eminently suitable for use on inland waters. The remainder of the range are powered by twin Perkins diesel engines and have a sea-going capability.

220: The Broom 35 European

Cheverton Workboats

Powered by a 15 h.p. Lister diesel, the **Champ's** standard open hull is ideal for beaching, for use as a rescue boat, a fishing boat or a ferry.

It can also be supplied with an open cabin in the forward part of the vessel (as illustrated). This is known as a 'cuddy'. While the company produces 20ft, 23ft and 24ft boats, perhaps the 27ft is the most versatile.

221: Cheverton Champ

L.O.A. 5·7m (18ft 11in)
Beam 2·28m (7ft 11in)
Approx weight
          1134kg (2500lb)

222: Cheverton 39

L.O.A. 12m (39ft)
Beam 3·6m (11ft 9in)
Draft 1·3m (4ft 6in)

Also known as the 40ft, the **Cheverton 39** gives a cruising speed of approximately 14 knots. Ideally suited for off-shore operations, she sees service as a medical launch; diving launch; water bus; fishing vessel and as a police launch. The illustration is of a police launch in Muscat.

223: Cleopatra 1000

L.O.A. 10m (33ft)
Beam 3·73m (12ft 3in)
Draft 1·21m (4ft)

The **Cleopatra 1000,** designed by Pelle Petersen, is the largest of the Cleopatra range which begins with the 700 Weekender, Sports Fisherman or family cruiser. She is powered by twin Volvo Penta engines which give her a range of 200 to 300 miles using some 440 litres (120 Imperial gal.). The quality of presentation from this company and full equipment list make this a desirable and well-liked family cruiser.

Coronet

The complete Coronet range consists of nine pleasure craft and numerous commercial craft. Built by Botved Boats of Denmark, the German Police use Coronet 21 for border patrol work; Coronet 31 Seafarer and the **Coronet 31** aft-cabin (which is illustrated) are also in production in Canada.

224: Coronet 31 (aft-cabin version)

L.O.A. 9·64m (31ft 8in)
Beam 3·18m (10ft 4in)
Draft 1·00m (3ft 3in)

Single Perkins Diesel HT6 354M or Twin Volvo Penta diesel MD 32 106 h.p.

163

225: Couach 1200

L.O.A. 12·00m (39ft 3in)
Beam 3·77m (12ft 3in)
Draft 0·85m (2ft 10in)
Twin diesel 210 s.h.p.
Displacement 6 tons

Categorized as a twin diesel express cruiser or 'fast motor yacht', the exceptional standard of construction and finish by the French builders of the **Couach** is noted in all the reports upon it. The company also build seven other types from the dayboat of 6·3m (20ft 8in) to a large 16·00m (52ft 6in) vessel.

Dell Quay (Dory)

This range of craft has established a world-wide reputation. From the Dory 11 Fisherman to the various 5·2m (17ft) hulls, the square plan shape and the triple 'V' hull are instantly recognizable. Safe and stable with immense inherent buoyancy (with an infinitely variable selection of power units, single or twin, depending on requirement) it is hardly surprising that an infinity of uses has been dreamed up for these craft.

Used by coastguards, as lifeboats, for air-sea rescue, as assault craft, for club rescue work and last but not least for pleasure, the variations are endless.

226: Testing the **Dory 13ft** for buoyancy whilst 'navigating'!
227: Demonstrating the **17ft Dell Quay Dory** equipped for military use (*right*)

228: Small but stable: the **Dell Quay 13ft Dory**

229: The **Dell Quay 17ft Dory**

Both **228** and **229** demonstrate the hull form of the Dell Quay range. Even in the 13ft (**228**) the very pronounced triple 'V' hull provides the ultimate in stability and the craft is extensively used in the United Kingdom as a rescue/safety boat for club and school sailing activities.

The Dell Quay Dory 17ft (**229**) is similarly very stable, but with a little more freeboard is not so suitable for retrieval of personnel from the water.

Draco

The range of Draco boats, initially designed for use among the Baltic skerries, has found a ready market throughout the world. The **2500 Flyfish,** with a moderate 'V' bottom, is admirably suited to partially sheltered waters. The smaller 2000 and 1700 are also well known, the 2000 taking first prize in the under 4-litre Class in 1973 Cowes–Torquay–Cowes Off-shore Race, winning a prize for fuel economy.

30: Draco 2500 Flyfish

O.A. 7·6m (24ft 11in)
eam 2·8m (9ft 2in)
raft 0·92m (3ft)
win petrol outdrives
20 s.h.p.
isplacement 2·57 tons

231 : Huntress 23

L.O.A. 7·04m (23ft)
Beam 2·59m (8ft 6i
Draft 0·84m (2ft 9i
Single diesel 145 s.h.p
Displacement 2·5 tons

Fairey Marine Ltd

Fairey high-speed diesel boats for leisure and commercial use range from 7m (23ft) to 19·6m (64ft). The policy of the company has been to develop the leisure craft for such commercial use and, worldwide, Fairey craft serve as police, customs, coastguard and air-sea rescue vessels.

With a maximum speed of 26 knots, and a range of 300 miles, **Huntress** has been used as a lifeboat as well as a family cruiser, and is here shown in a Naval role.

Spear is developed from the pleasure craft Spearfish and is the fastest diesel Police or Customs boat of her size. She has a maximum speed of 28 knots. The 'dome' on her coachroof is part of the radar equipment. The Spearfish (not illustrated) is slightly lighter but sufficiently robust to circumnavigate the two main islands of Japan in 16 days without incident in heavy weather!

232 : Spear

L.O.A. 9·1m (30ft)
Beam 2·75m (9ft)
Draft 0·84m (2ft 9in
Twin diesel 180 s.h.p.
Displacement 4·7 tons

233: Fantôme

L.O.A. 9·81m (32ft 2½in)
Beam 2·97m (9ft 9in)
Draft 0·86m (2ft 10in)
Twin diesel 180 s.h.p.
Displacement 4·75 tons

234: Super Swordsman

L.O.A. 10m (33ft)
Beam 3·48m (11ft 5in)
Draft 0·9m (3ft)
Twin diesel 180 s.h.p.
Displacement 6·5 tons

Fantôme is the latest version of the famous Huntsman 31 with similar fine entry and flared bows based on race design practice. With a reputation for seakeeping and fast passage-making, Fantôme will cruise at 20 knots in the normal rough waters off the United Kingdom.

Twin 6-cylinder turbo-charged diesel engines drive the **Super Swordsman** which won the All-Rounder prize for two years in succession in the International Offshore Powerboat Race.

Built as a Fast Coastguard Patrol Boat, the **Tracker,** a 19·6m (64ft) twin 690 h.p. diesel craft, is in use for many official duties. Credited with a maximum speed of 25 knots, her range is 500 miles at 15 knots.

235: Tracker

236: The very successful **Fletcher 'Arrow-
shaft'** at speed

237: The Glastron
15ft petrol outboard
sportsboat

Fletcher Marine/Glastron

Norman Fletcher, the well-known international offshore powerboat racing driver, heads a firm which
produces consistently high standard craft. The
'Arrowshaft' set the pattern in 1972, competing very
successfully in world championships. Glastron
(U.K.) Ltd produces a range of highly competitive
ski/sports boats which are marketed by the Fletcher
Marine company in addition to the Fletcher craft
headed by the race-successful 'Arrowshaft'.

238 depicts the Glastron craft equipped with a 330
h.p. Oldsmobile engine coupled to a Berkeley Jet
Unit. This jet-driven vessel can travel at more than
50 knots. At high speeds the manœuvrability of this
craft is excellent. At lower speeds, the water-jet drive
loses a little in steerage capability.

238: The Glastron
with jet-drive propul-
sion

39: Grand Banks 32

L.O.A. 9·73m (31ft)
Beam 3·40m (11ft 6in)
Draft 1·13m (3ft 9in)
Displacement 7·58 tons

40: Grand Banks 36

L.O.A. 11·07m (36ft 4in)
Beam 3·71m (12ft 2in)
Draft 1·69m (3ft 11in)

Grand Banks Diesel Cruisers

The whole range of Grand Banks Diesel Cruisers are especially designed for long-distance cruising and for fishing. The 36, 42, 48 and 50 have dual steering positions, either from the wheelhouse or from the flying bridge.

All are powered by highly efficient marinized diesel engines, provide considerable accommodation on board according to their various sizes, and are renowned for their fine construction and reliability.

These craft are produced by American Marine Ltd of Costa Mesa, California, and range in size from 32ft (9·73m) to 50ft (15·5m).

241: Grand Banks 48

L.O.A. 14·8m (48ft 6in)
Beam 4·7m (15ft 5in)
Draft 1·4m (4ft 6in)

242: Moonraker 36

L.O.A. 11·00m (36ft 1in)
Beam 3·51m (11ft 6in)
Draft 0·92m (3ft)
Twin 180 h.p. diesels

243: Newhaven Sea Angler 31

L.O.A. 9·46m (31ft)
Beam 3·36m (11ft)
Draft 0·92m (3ft)
Single inboard diesel 120 s.h.p.

The **Moonraker 36** is one of the most successful express cruisers built in the United Kingdom to an excellent specification. Robert Tucker has collaborated as designer to the company for a number of years. There are various optional layouts including a fly-bridge and a large open after cockpit.

The **Newhaven Sea Angler,** a glassfibre-hulled craft, has excellent sea-keeping performance. She is a traditional displacement craft.

Northshore

Two craft marketed by this company are of interest to the observer. The **Ranger 36** is a six-berth express diesel cruiser. Designed by PACEurope, the Rum Runner 27 (not illustrated) is a high-speed weekend cruiser with a large well-sheltered cockpit.

244: The Ranger 36 marketed by Northshore Yachts

Powles 41, 38 and 33

Powles International Marine range of coastal cruisers includes the **41**; with dual control from the fly-bridge or the wheelhouse. The craft is luxuriously equipped and powered by twin Perkins or Volvo, according to taste. Sensibly handled, she provides completely safe and comfortable cruising, travelling at semi-displacement speeds. The 38 (not illustrated), equally luxurious, can be fitted with 175 s.h.p. engines as standard or the larger 250 s.h.p. The Powles 33 (not illustrated), designed for the company by Bernard Olesinski, is powered by twin GM Bedford 466M engines giving a cruising speed of around 19 knots and a range of some 225 miles.

Princess 37, 32 and 25

The **Princess 32** is in the middle of a range of medium priced power cruisers which have been successfully produced in considerable quantities by Marine Projects of Plymouth, England. She is powered by twin 105 s.h.p. diesel engines. The Princess 25 (not illustrated) was introduced in 1974.

246: The **Princess 32**, one of a range of medium priced cruisers

171

247:
The Riva 2000

48: The Riva 45—
Superamerica

Riva

The **Riva 2000,** with a length overall of 11·30m (approx. 36ft), is powered by three 350 h.p. engines and 'surface' propellers. Such power and the special design of the propellers which are not totally immersed like a conventional propeller, provides this craft (which weighs more than 6 tons) with a maximum speed suited to its looks. The Riva company has been known for more than thirty years for its craftsmanship in wood and it is only comparatively recently that the company has produced a fine range of fibreglass boats. The smallest in the range is the Rudy (a ski-boat) and the largest is the **Superamerica.** Of Italian design she is powered by twin diesels producing top speeds of around 30 knots.

The **Seahound** is marketed in England by J.G. Meakes Ltd, and was designed by Leonardo da Costa Saiago. The twin GM Bedford diesel engines give a cruising speed in excess of 20 knots, with a range of approximately 300 miles.

249: Seahound

L.O.A. 9·45m (31ft 2in)
Beam 3·38m (11ft 1in)
Draft 0·56m (1ft 10in)
Twin diesel 146 s.h.p.
Displacement 4·25 tons

250: The Shetland Family Four which is frequently seen in the United Kingdom and Europe

251: The Shetland 570 is ideal as a small family dayboat cruiser

Shetland

The Shetland Boat Company of Bury St Edmunds, England, produces a wide range of sports boats varying in length from the smallest which is 4·57m (15ft) in length. The 535 is perhaps the most widely known small cruiser in Europe.

Sunseeker (Poole Powerboats, England)

The Sunseeker, developed as a dayboat cruiser, has a cruising range of 130 miles. An alternative interior design is called the Rio S 20.

252: S20 Sunseeker

L.O.A. 6·3m (20ft)
Beam 2·28m (7ft 7in)
Draft 0·71m (2ft 4in)
Stern drive inboard
           130 s.h.p.
Displacement 1 ton

253: Tremlett 30 Sport

L.O.A. 9·15m (30ft)
Beam 3·66m (12ft)
Draft 0·76m (2ft 6in)
Twin 180 h.p. Sabre marine
diesel engines

254: Tremlett 21 Sport

L.O.A. 6·41m (21ft)
Beam 2·29m (7ft 6in)
Draft 0·61m (2ft)

255: Sandy Bay Girl
(by Tremlett Ltd)

L.O.A. 10·07m (33ft)
Beam 3·20m (10ft 6in)
Draft 0·61m (2ft)
Twin Perkins diesels
developing 250 h.p. each

Tremlett Ltd

An example from the large range built by this British company, the **Tremlett 30 Sports** has a cruising range of 14 hours. With an exceptionally deep 'V' hull she is stable in choppy sea conditions.

Capable of being fitted with various power units the **Tremlett 21 Sports** is a fine example of the smaller craft in this production series.

Sandy Bay Girl is illustrated because of her particular interest as a 'trendsetter'. She gained the World Speed Record for cabin boats in 1975, propelled by 'super-cavitating' surface propellers. This idea may well extend to cruising craft. Only half the propeller is immersed in the smooth water under the stern of the craft. The design gives considerably improved efficiency and a 'streamlining' of effort which improves performance.

174

256: Pisces 45

L.O.A. 13·73m (45ft)
Beam 4·12m (13ft 6in)
Draft 1·19m (3ft 10in)
Twin 375 h.p. Caterpillar
diesels

257: 40ft Vigia

T.T. Boat Designs

Commander Peter Thornycroft is responsible for the design and completion of a highly successful range of planing round-bilge boats used not only for pleasure but by Port Authorities; Customs; pilot service; police work and Coastguard surveillance.

The **Pisces 45** illustrated acted as the start boat in the 1973 Cowes–Torquay Race and subsequently went on service as *Skawpilot II* based at Skagen on the northern tip of Denmark.

The **40ft Vigia** was one of the first Halmatic 40ft (12·2m) hulls (to a Thornycroft design) extensively used by Trinity House while based at the Ryde, Isle of Wight, Pilot Station.

Horatia 40 (258) is powered by twin 400 h.p. Caterpillar diesels. This craft competed in many long-distance powerboat races and is illustrated at the start of the Round Britain Race (*below*).

259: Capricorn

L.O.A. 5·5m (18ft)
Beam 2·1m (7ft)
Draft 0·53m (1ft 9in)
Powered by various
petrol outdrive engines
(230 s.h.p.)

260: Scorpio

L.O.A. 4·57m (15ft)
Beam 1·8m (5ft 11in)
Draft 0·49m (1ft 6in)
Powered by petrol
outboard

261: Gemini

L.O.A. 3·9m (12ft 6in)
Beam 1·6m (5ft 4in)
Approx weight 156kg
(345lb)

Zodiac ski-boats

Jack Broom is the designer and builder of a number of top-quality ski-boats.

The maximum speed of **Capricorn** is about 47 knots; quite sufficient to provide this good seaboat with skiing potential. She is the largest of the Jack Broom Zodiac fleet.

Scorpio won awards at the London International Boat Show, as did her 'sister ship' the Capricorn. Another excellent example from this prolific designer.

The smallest of the range from Zodiac, **Gemini** is designed to take short-shaft outboards of around 50 h.p. and is a standard 'run-about' of a kind frequently seen in United Kingdom waters.

Appendix I

A GLOSSARY OF SAILING TERMS

Abaft Nearer to the stern than anything else.

Abeam At right-angles to the fore-and-aft line of a craft.

About (going) When a vessel's bows pass through the wind.

Accommodation Sleeping and domestic space aboard a craft.

Aft Towards, at or near the stern.

After part That part of the craft near the stern.

Ahull (lying) When a vessel is stripped of sail in bad weather.

Alee To leeward, away from the wind or downwind.

Aloft Above the deck.

Amidships Centred helm; dead centre; the middle of a craft.

Anemometer Instrument for measuring wind strength.

Antifouling Paint for underwater surfaces (applied to prevent marine growth).

Astern Behind, in the direction of the stern of a vessel.

Athwart Across the vessel's width.

Awash Beneath the surface, or washed over by water.

Bail To remove water from a craft.

Ballast Weight below the deck in hull to counteract top weight or wind pressure on the sails.

Bar Shoal or shallows formed across a river mouth.

Batten Flexible piece of wood, metal or plastic at the **leech** of the sail to prevent curl. **Batten pocket,** slot to accommodate a batten in a sail.

Beam The extreme width of a vessel.

Beam sea A sea striking the vessel at right-angles.

Bear away To alter course away from the wind or another vessel.

Beat A sailing craft is beating when close-hauled to **windward.**

Becalmed Deprived of wind.

Bend A form of knot to attach a rope to a bar, spar or ring.

Bend on To put a sail on a spar, or one rope to another.

Bermudan A form of rig (fore and aft) without gaff or yard.

Berth A sleeping place on board. To bring a craft alongside a dock or quay.

Bight A loop in a rope.

Bilge The curve of the bottom of a vessel or the space beneath the cabin sole. **Bilge keel** One of two keels fixed to the side of the bottom of a vessel.

Block Pulley incorporating a grooved wheel over which any **running rigging** may pass.

Bobstay Chain or wire to restrain upward pull upon the bowsprit.

Bollard Drum-shaped post on a quay to which mooring lines may be fixed.

Boom Any horizontal spar to which the foot of a sail is affixed.

Bottle screw Screw-threaded barrel, with a threaded eye at each end, to tension rigging.

Bowline Knot used to tie a **bight** in a rope.

Bulkhead Any transverse partition within a hull.

Burgee Triangular masthead flag indicating membership or ownership.

Cable Chain connecting the anchor to a craft. 200yd (182·880m) distance.

Cast off To let go a vessel from a quay or mooring.

Centreboard Hinged or sliding movable keel of a sailing craft fitted to provide lateral resistance.

Cleat T-shaped fitting to which a rope is secured.
Clew The lower after corner of a triangular sail. Either lower corner of a square sail.
Cockpit Well in which the crew of a sailing craft work when not on deck.
Compass Instrument used to indicate position relative to a meridian.
Cringle Metal reinforced hole in a sail.
Crosstrees Struts fixed to spread the **shrouds** to support the mast.

Dead eye Any D-shaped or circular fitting through which a rope may be secured.
Dead reckoning Plot of a vessel's position by course steered and distance run. Correctly 'deduced reckoning'.
Deck log Record noted in a book of all alterations of course, speed, time etc.
Dogwatch Two two-hour watches of duty between 4 p.m. and 6 p.m. and 6 p.m. and 8 p.m.
Dress overall To display International Code Flags and wear from stem to stern over the masthead on special occasions.

Ebb The receding tide.
Eight bells The end of a **Watch.**
Ensign Maritime flag worn to denote a vessel's nationality.

Fairlead Eye or other fitting through which a rope is passed to alter its direction.
Fairway Navigable part of a channel.
Fetch To reach a destination without having to **tack.**
Flotsam Goods lost overboard by mistake. (*cf.* **Jetsam**.)
Fly The horizontal length of a flag.
Foot Lower edge of a sail.
Forestay Wire rope from masthead to bow.

For'ard Forward, opposite of **aft**.

Furl To fold, roll or gather up a sail.

Galley The 'kitchen' on board any vessel.

Ghosting Sailing in light airs with light sails.

Gooseneck Fitting attaching the boom to the mast.

Goose-wing To sail downwind with mainsail set on one side and headsail on the other.

Gunwale The uppermost edge of a vessel's side.

Gybe To bring the wind through the stern (when running) so that the boom swings to the opposite tack.

Halyard Rope or wire used for hoisting a sail or flag.

Hank Clip to hold the **luff** of a sail to a stay. **Hank on** The act of clipping the luff to a stay.

Headboard Strengthened piece of sail at the head of a triangular mainsail.

Heave-to To back the jib and adjust the mainsail to hold a sailing craft stationary.

Heel To lie over, to list.

Helm Tiller or wheel.

In irons A sailing craft is said to be 'in irons' when it will not 'pay off' on to either tack.

Jetsam Goods deliberately thrown overboard. (*cf.* **Flotsam**.)

Kedge A light anchor, generally used with a rope.

Kicking strap Rope or tackle to restrain the boom from lifting.

Knot The joining of ropes. A measure of speed; one nautical mile per hour.

Lee The side farthest from the wind.

Leech The after edge of a sail.

Lee shore Shore on to which the wind is blowing.

Leeward The sheltered side of a ship. In the direction to which the wind is blowing. (*cf.* **Windward**.)

Leeway Sideways movement of a craft.

L.O.A. (abbrev.) length overall.

Luff The forward edge of a sail. To turn closer into the wind.

Make fast To secure any rope.

Neap Tides between full and new moon with less range than spring tides.

Painter Rope attached to the bow of a dinghy.

Patent log Measuring instrument to show the distance run.

Pennant Any pointed flag except a **burgee**.

Port Left-hand side of a vessel. A round window.

Port tack, when a sailing craft has the wind on the left side.

Quarter After-part of the side of a craft. **Quarter berth,** bunk half-under the cockpit deck.

Range Vertical distance between high and low tide.

Reef To reduce the area of sail. **Reef-knot,** one with interlocking bights.

Reeve To pass a rope through a fairlead, block or dead-eye.

Riding light White anchor light in the forepart of a vessel.

Rowlock A U-shaped fitting for an oar.

Rudder stock Part of the rudder which is closest to the stern.

Running rigging Movable sheet, halyard or rope. (*cf.* **Standing rigging**.)

Shackle U-shaped piece of metal with an open mouth closed by a bar.

S.h.p. Shaft horse power.

Sheet A rope to trim sail. **Sheet home,** to haul a sheet taut. **Sheet in,** to trim a sail.

Shroud Wire rope to support a mast, from mast-head to side deck.

Slack water The 'pause' between high and low water.

Slick A smooth patch of water caused by the hull or a deposit of oil.

Spitfire jib Smallest headsail for use in heavy weather.

Spreaders Lateral spars on the mast to spread the rigging for strength.

Spring Mooring line to restrain a craft from forward and backward movement.

Standing rigging Permanent rigging to support a mast.

Starboard Right-hand side of vessel viewed from the stern; **Starboard tack,** sailing with the wind on the starboard side.

Stay Wire rope for fore-and-aft support of the mast.

Stem Main timber at the bow of a vessel.

Stern The aftermost part of any craft.

Stern post The aftermost part of a vessel where the rudder is attached.

Tabernacle Fitting on deck into which the mast heel is fitted.

Tack The lower forward corner of a fore-and-aft sail. The act of putting the vessel **about.**

Tang A metal fitting to which rigging is attached.

Thwart A seat across a vessel's breadth.

Tiller The bar by which the helmsman controls the rudder.

Topping lift A rope (uphaul) to support the boom end when a sail is not completely set.

Transom The flat stern of a sailing craft.

Trysail A small mainsail set in heavy weather.

Una rig This rig consists of a single mainsail.

Under way Term used when a craft is moving.

Union 'Jack' The Union Flag surrounded by a white border.

Wake The disturbance of water left by a vessel under way.

Warp Loosely used term to denote any mooring lines.

Watch Period, usually 4 hours, for which each section of the crew is on duty. (*cf.* **Dogwatch**.)

Weigh To raise the anchor.

Windward In the direction from which the wind is blowing.

Yard A spar to which a square sail or top-sail is bent.

Zephyr A soft, gentle breeze.

APPENDIX II

AN ALPHABETICAL LIST OF SAILING CRUISERS AND OFFSHORE RACERS IN THIS BOOK

Appendix III
AN ALPHABETICAL LIST OF

DAYBOATS WITH THEIR SAIL
INSIGNIA (IF ANY)

Appendix IV

AN ALPHABETICAL LIST OF POWERED CRAFT

Appendix V

INTERNATIONAL SAIL LETTERS DENOTING THE COUNTRY TO WHICH A SAILING CRAFT BELONGS

A	Argentine
B	Belgium
BA	Bahamas
BL	Brazil
D	Denmark
E	Spain
F	France
G	West Germany
GO	East Germany
GR	Greece
H	Holland
I	Italy
IR	Eire
J	Japan
K	United Kingdom
KA	Australia
KB	Bermuda
KC	Canada
KJ	Jamaica
KR	Rhodesia
KZ	New Zealand

L	Finland
M	Hungary
Mo	Monaco
MX	Mexico
N	Norway
OE	Austria
P	Portugal
PH	Philippines
PK	Pakistan
PR	Puerto Rico
PZ	Poland
S	Sweden
SA	South Africa
SR	U.S.S.R.
TH	Thailand
US	U.S.A.
V	Venezuela
VI	Virgin Islands
Y	Yugoslavia
Z	Switzerland

INDEX

The page upon which individual boats appear is shown in the Appendices. Appendix II lists sailing cruisers and offshore racers, Appendix III lists Dayboats and Appendix IV powerboats.